Endorsements for Future for Latino Church

"Daniel Rodriguez's *A Future for the Latino Church* is a truly informative and inspiring book. Based on solid theological, demographic and sociological research from the perspective of the author's own cultural and spiritual pilgrimage, this book presents a compelling argument for reaching U.S.-born Latinos with the gospel message. The carefully selected case studies of highly effective transgenerational Latino churches provide valuable insights as well as a clear sense of direction regarding the future of Latino work in this country. I wholeheartedly recommend this book to everyone who is interested in seeing America's fastest-growing ethnic group become a missionary force in this country and throughout the world."

Daniel R. Sánchez, author of *Hispanic Realities Impacting America* and director of the Scarborough Institute of Church Planting & Growth, Southwestern Baptist Theological Seminary

"*A Future for the Latino Church* is an attempt by my good friend Daniel Rodriguez to awaken us to two realities: the coming 'Joseph' generation which looks differently, acts differently and speaks differently, but is nevertheless Hispanic and potentially the hope for revival in America; and secondly, the reality of crosscultural pollination that is occurring within every ethnic group in the second, third and fourth generations in this country."

Rev. Daniel de León, senior pastor, Templo Calvario, Santa Ana, CA

"For decades native-born, English-speaking Latinos have endured the neglect of their spiritual and cultural formation at the hands of Spanish-dominant Latino church leaders who refused change that would address the needs of this growing population of Latinos in the United States. Dr. Rodriguez clearly articulates the resistance present and the transitional shift needed for holistic English-language ministry to flourish in the lives of second-generation Latinos. Every Christian leader who is serious about understanding the complexity and diversity of Latinos must read this insightful contribution to the advancement of the gospel to all Latinos and to the future of the church as a whole in America."

Rev. Orlando Crespo, national director of InterVarsity Latino Fellowship and author of *Being Latino in* Christ

"*A Future for the Latino Church* takes you 'back to the future' of Hispanic ministry in the United States. It is about the growing second and third generations of English-dominant Hispanics who represent a kind of *nepantla*, an Aztec Indian word for both/and, of in-betweenness in American life. Memory and destiny frame the five paradoxes in the life of Hispanics of 'living in the hyphen,' that is, two languages (Spanish/English), two cultures (native/American), two philosophies (indigeneous/contemporary), two strategies (tradition/missional) and even two religions (Catholic/Evangelical) competing as the twins in Rebecca's womb, constituting the challenge of ministering to future generations of Hispanics. This book highlights some groundbreaking creative, holistic yet prophetic ministries that have begun to steer the way toward the future of Hispanic ministry in the United States."

Dr. Jesse Miranda, president, The Miranda Center, and CEO, National Hispanic Christian Leadership Conference

"English-dominant Latinos have great capacity to strengthen churches everywhere. But these Latinos are neglected by church leaders who are fixated on the idea that the only authentic Hispanic ministry is Spanish-language ministry. Dr. Daniel Rodriguez's research into effective multilingual, multicultural churches demonstrates how churches and individuals can draw, nurture and activate this vital group."

Rodolpho Carrasco, board member, World Vision USA, and director, Two Forty Group

"Daniel Rodriguez challenges us to recognize the increasing diversity of the Latino community and to develop ministries that reach out across that diversity. He also provides examples of churches that are developing models to respond to that challenge. Latino churches have an important future in the United States. Rodriguez helps us understand an important part of that future."

Juan Francisco Martínez, Fuller Theological Seminary, and author, *Walk with the People: Latino Ministry in the United States*

"Daniel Rodriguez presents the framework for twenty-first-century Hispanic American Christian viability and sustainability. As one of the most prominent Hispanic scholars in the church, Daniel captures both the obstacles and opportunities embedded within America's fastest-growing segment of Christianity, Hispanic evangelicals. This book contextualizes the narrative of successful church models that engage, empower and enrich multiple generations for the glory of Christ. Every pastor and church leader committed to reaching the Hispanic American demographic must read this book."

Rev. Samuel Rodriguez, president, National Hispanic Christian Leadership Conference, The Hispanic National Association of Evangelicals

DANIEL A. RODRIGUEZ

Foreword by Manuel Ortiz

A FUTURE FOR THE LATINO CHURCH

Models for Multilingual, Multigenerational Hispanic Congregations

IVP Academic

An imprint of InterVarsity Press
Downers Grove, Illinois

InterVarsity Press
P.O. Box 1400, Downers Grove, IL 60515-1426
World Wide Web: www.ivpress.com
E-mail: email@ivpress.com

InterVarsity Press® is the book-publishing division of InterVarsity Christian Fellowship/USA®, a movement of students and faculty active on campus at hundreds of universities, colleges and schools of nursing in the United States of America, and a member movement of the International Fellowship of Evangelical Students. For information about local and regional activities, write Public Relations Dept., InterVarsity Christian Fellowship/USA, 6400 Schroeder Rd., P.O. Box 7895, Madison, WI 53707-7895, or visit the IVCF website at <www.intervarsity.org>.

Cover design: Cindy Kiple
Interior design: Beth Hagenberg
Images: graham klotz/iStockphoto

ISBN 978-0-8308-3930-8

Printed in the United States of America ∞

Library of Congress Cataloging-in-Publication Data

Rodriguez, Daniel A., 1955-
  A future for the Latino church: models for multilingual,
multigenerational Hispanic congregations/Daniel A. Rodriguez.
       p.cm.
  Includes bibliographical references (p.   ) and index.
  ISBN 978-0-8308-3930-8 (pbk.: alk. paper)
  1. Hispanic American churches. I. Title.
  BR563.H57R63 2011
  277.3'08308968—dc22

2011006815

P	20	19	18	17	16	15	14	13	12	11	10	9	8	7	6	5	4	3	2	1
Y	28	27	26	25	24	23	22	21	20	19	18	17	16	15	14	13	12	11			

To Jeanette,

my devoted and encouraging wife and friend

CONTENTS

FOREWORD

A Future for the Latino Church is an important book for all who are concerned about the mission of the church in the context of urbanization and globalization. Communities, especially in urban centers, are undergoing rapid transitions. Immigrant groups are emerging from all corners of the world. Folks who once lived in areas of the city where gentrification is occurring have been relocated and now live on the outskirts of the city. Even as I write this foreword many of the communities listed in this book are being replaced with mostly Anglo professionals, such as uptown Manhattan, New York City, where mostly African Americans, Puerto Ricans and Dominicans once lived, and Humboldt Park, Chicago, where Hispanics once lived and have had to move outside the city to areas such as Waukegan, Illinois.

Another transition is that neighborhoods once filled with first-generation immigrants are now bilingual and are becoming more and more English speaking. Churches in these neighborhoods are also recognizing this movement within their congregations. The original immigrants' often monolingual churches, primarily utilizing their mother tongue, now have to deal with an English-speaking second (and beyond) generation who prefer services in English. This is not a new trend, as immigrant groups from Europe in the early twentieth century eventually found their children using English as their primary language. If this phenomenon is not anticipated, many of these younger people will move out and find more suitable churches. How should the church respond to this mission call?

This mission challenge is not new to the Hispanic church, but is one that was written about in my book *The Hispanic Challenge* (1993). Daniel Rodriguez provides significant information and strategy to approach this missional challenge successfully. Movements are inevitable, and mission concerns for the church must take precedence. This important book attempts to instill in the Hispanic church a missional mindset to be proactive in developing a strategy to prepare second-generation emerging leaders to be effective leaders within the context of the Hispanic church and community. The Hispanic church can and should truly make an impact on our cities. The Hispanic church has always been passionate about evangelism; however, it may have side-stepped other ethnic groups and English-speaking Hispanics. Stephen Arroyo, in his book *Prophets Denied Honor* (1980), notes that the evangelization of young Puerto Ricans, as difficult as it may be for any traditional missionary approach, may well hold the key to the future of Christianity in New York City.

In this century the key to evangelizing Latinos entering and leaving the United States will be for missionary-minded churches to creatively bring Christ into these transitioning communities. At the same time, the key to growing the Hispanic church, and leaders who are English speaking and bilingual and capable of crossing cultures without departing from their culture, will be a willingness to utilize and empower young and capable men and women for the task of an urban and global mission.

I know the relevance of this book will touch not only Hispanics but also other language groups, such as the Korean and Chinese churches. We are all losing many of our emerging leaders to other congregations because too often we are unwilling to make cultural transitions. I am delighted with the hard work and devotion of Daniel Rodriguez presented in this book, which will help us get on with the Great Commission.

Manuel Ortiz

LIST OF TABLES AND FIGURES

ACKNOWLEDGMENTS

The writing of this book was made possible by many people and institutions that I feel privileged to gratefully acknowledge. This study reflects many hours in dialogue with busy, dedicated denominational leaders, local pastors, ministers and lay leaders engaged in cutting-edge Hispanic ministry across the United States. I gratefully acknowledge the invaluable contribution made by dozens of church leaders who candidly shared their struggles, successes, setbacks and dreams with me, and for providing added credibility, depth and relevance to this book. For access to many of the people, churches and ministries described in this book, I am especially indebted to Reverend Samuel Rodríguez, president of the National Hispanic Christian Leadership Conference, and Dr. Jesse Miranda, chair of the World Hispanic Evangelical Alliance. Experts in Hispanic ministry from across the country, including professors Manuel Ortiz and Daniel R. Sánchez, contributed sage advice and helped me identify and clarify many sensitive cultural and theological issues and concerns addressed in this study. Similarly, the outside readers for InterVarsity Press provided critical comments steering me clear of many pitfalls, especially when describing and analyzing the tension and cultural conflict that often exists between foreign-born and native-born Latinos in the context of the local church. It was also my distinct pleasure to work with Al Hsu, my editor at InterVarsity Press, who offered invaluable insights, guidance and encouragement.

Just as important, research for this book was made possible by several generous grants from the Dean's Office at Pepperdine University's Seaver College of Letters, Arts, and Sciences. Likewise, many colleagues, especially in the Religion Division at Pepperdine University, were a constant source of encouragement throughout the writing process.

Last but not least, I want to gratefully recognize my wife, Jeanette, for her unswerving confidence in the Lord Jesus Christ and in me, his servant. Her love, patience and encouragement were by far my greatest source of human strength. Above all, I am grateful to my Lord and Savior Jesus Christ, who has richly blessed my life in order that I in turn can be a blessing to others, especially those committed to preaching the gospel to all the nations (Ps 67). May this study better equip Christ's church to share the gospel in culturally relevant ways in the power of the Holy Spirit and thereby participate more effectively in the mission of God the Father—"to gather up all things in [Christ], things in heaven and things on earth" (Eph 1:10).

INTRODUCTION

A MOMENT OF TRANSITION IN THE BARRIO

Now during those days, when the disciples were increasing
in number, the Hellenists complained against the Hebrews because their
widows were being neglected in the daily distribution of food.

ACTS 6:1

SHORTLY AFTER THEIR DELIVERANCE from Egyptian bondage the people tested the Lord, grumbling against his servant Moses because
they had no water to drink. Moses is instructed by the Lord, "Strike
the rock, and water will come out of it, so that the people may drink"
(Ex 17:6). Forty years later, Numbers 20:1-13 describes a similar situation when a "second generation" of Israelites grumbles against Moses
because there is no water to drink. Once more God instructs Moses
to take his staff and leads him to a rock. However, this time the in-
structions are modified slightly. Instead of striking the rock, Moses is
instructed to "command the rock," which will then produce water to
quench the people's thirst. Unfortunately, Moses fails to recognize
what Dave Serrano, pastor at *Iglesia Cristiana Tesalónica* in the South
Bronx, calls "the moment of transition."[1] Instead, with heart-break-
ing results Moses does what he was accustomed to doing: he strikes
the rock. Moses may have been the first pastor to coin the phrase,
"But we've never done it like that before!"

The familiar episode described above raises an important question:

---

[1]Dave Serrano, interview with author, May 21, 2008.

Do leaders and members of Hispanic churches in the United States recognize that their communities are also in a moment of transition? Older barrios in cities like Chicago, Dallas, Los Angeles, Houston, Miami, New York, Philadelphia and San Antonio, once dominated by foreign-born[2] Spanish-speaking *mexicanos, cubanos* and *puertoriqueños*, are now dominated by their native-born[3] children and grandchildren. Even more significantly, a growing number of U.S.-born Latinos are not only English dominant, but they do not speak Spanish at all! Furthermore, they often do not maintain the same level of allegiance to their ancestral homelands or to the cultural and religious commitments their parents or grandparents brought with them from their countries of origin. Nevertheless, the overwhelming majority of U.S.-born English-dominant Latinos are still Latinos at heart. However, they embrace many values and attributes of the dominant group in the United States, thereby creating a cultural distance between themselves and their foreign-born parents, grandparents and neighbors who have more recently arrived in the United States from Latin America and the Caribbean. This book seeks to address this reality in a way that not only helps to inform and equip the Hispanic evangelical church to fulfill its God-given mission but also in a way that strengthens Hispanic families and communities across the country, especially those being impacted by this moment of transition.

U.S.-BORN LATINOS: MODERN-DAY HELLENISTIC JEWS

From *el barrio* in Spanish Harlem to the *calles* of East L.A., from Little Havana in Miami to Humboldt Park in Chicago and in many places in between, Latino disciples are increasing in number! This is very good news! However, the history of the early church reminds us that as the church begins to grow, so will the problems it faces. For those of us who find ourselves in the midst of Hispanic communities once dominated by Spanish-speaking immigrants and now filled with increasing num-

---

[2]*Foreign-born, first-generation* and *immigrant-generation* will be used interchangeably throughout this study to refer to all individuals of Latin American ancestry who have legally or illegally immigrated to the United States.

[3]*Native-born, U.S.-born,* and *second-* and *third-generation* all refer to individuals of Latin American ancestry who were born in the United States.

bers of native-born English-dominant Latinos, the episode described in Acts 6:1-7 is instructive.

In Acts 6:1 we are told, "Now during those days, when the disciples were increasing in number, the Hellenists complained against the Hebrews because their widows were being neglected in the daily distribution of food." When Luke tells us that the "Hellenists" (*Hellēnistēs* in Greek) were complaining against the "Hebrews" (*Hebraios* in Greek) he is giving us the first glimpse into the cultural diversity found in the earliest Christian community. But who are the *Hellēnistai* and the *Hebraioi* mentioned in this passage? New Testament scholars are almost unanimous in identifying the "Hellenists" mentioned in Acts 6:1 with "Greek-speaking Jewish Christians" rather than with "Greek-speaking Gentiles." The "Hebrews" refers to "Aramaic-speaking Jews."[4] This means that the distinction between the *Hellēnistai* and the *Hebraioi* in Acts 6:1 appears to be linguistic rather than ethnic. The "Hellenists" were Jews who predominantly spoke Greek and had been influenced to varying degrees by Greek culture. Based on earlier references in Acts (see Acts 2:7-12; 4:36; 6:9) some were probably from the Diaspora,[5] but others would have been from Palestine, where Greek was widely spoken among Jews. Of course, the "Hebrews" refers to Aramaic-speaking Jews who were natives of Palestine.[6]

Evidently the daily distribution of food mentioned in Acts 4:35 was not being carried out equitably. The Aramaic-speaking Jews responsible for the distribution of food were somehow overlooking the Greek-speaking widows, prompting the complaint of the Hellenists. We are not told explicitly the reason the Greek-speaking widows were overlooked. The neglect of the Hellenistic widows seems to be the unintentional outcome of the rapid growth of the church (Acts 6:1), growth that required more attention than the twelve apostles could provide.[7] We are then told that the apostles "called together the whole community of the disciples" to address the crisis. The complaint of the Greek-

---

[4]Joseph A. Fitzmyer, *The Acts of the Apostles* (New York: Doubleday, 1998), pp. 347-48.
[5]Then as now, "the Diaspora" most commonly refers to the Jewish population found in Gentile lands.
[6]Luke T. Johnson, *The Acts of the Apostles* (Collegeville, Minn.: Liturgical Press, 1992), p. 105.
[7]Beverly Roberts Gaventa, *The Acts of the Apostles* (Nashville: Abingdon, 2003), p. 114.

speaking Jews against the Aramaic-speaking Jews is heard by everyone. The problem is acknowledged and a creative solution is proposed. The apostles direct the Hellenists to select seven respected, Spirit-filled and wise men to take over the task of distributing food to the needy. It is noteworthy that with the exception of "Nicolaus, a proselyte" (i.e., a convert to Judaism), all the men are Hellenistic Jews.[8] We are also told that Nicolaus is from Antioch, a city that figures prominently in Luke's narrative beginning in Acts 11:19. Some scholars believe that mention of his non-Palestinian origin suggests that the others are indeed Hellenistic Jews *from* Palestine.[9] The seven men are then publicly ordained and appointed to their task. In response to the apostles' proposal, Luke adds, "the whole community" including Hellenists and Hebrews was pleased. Then as a sign of the Lord's endorsement, "The word of God continued to spread; the number of the disciples increased greatly in Jerusalem, and a great many of the priests became obedient to the faith" (Acts 6:7).

My research during the past five years has convinced me that a modern-day parallel to the episode described in Acts 6:1-7 is being played out in barrios in Chicago, Dallas/Fort Worth, Los Angeles, Miami, New York, Philadelphia and San Antonio. With the rapid growth of the Hispanic evangelical church during the past three decades, problems have arisen. One of the most significant is that U.S.-born English-dominant Latinos are unintentionally being overlooked in the distribution of the church's attention and resources. U.S.-born English-dominant Latinos, the modern-day Hellenists, are grumbling against foreign-born Spanish-dominant Latinos, the modern-day Hebrews. The complaint of the former is that many Spanish-dominant Latinos still equate "Hispanic ministry" with ministry conducted almost exclusively in Spanish. Under this assumption and historic paradigm, generations of U.S.-born English-dominant Latinos are subsequently "being overlooked in the daily distribution" of *spiritual* food.

Unfortunately, it is not possible to call together "the whole *comunidad de discípulos*" to become aware of and address the challenges facing

---

[8]Fitzmyer, *Acts of the Apostles*, p. 350.
[9]Roberts Gaventa, *Acts of the Apostles*, p. 115.

the Hispanic evangelical church in the early twenty-first century. Instead, I have tried to listen carefully to Latino evangelical leaders from across the country in an effort to understand the nature of the challenges facing our communities and the churches that serve them. I have also had the privilege of meeting wise and prayerful modern-day "apostles" among foreign-born Spanish-dominant Latinos, men and women who have been appointed by God to distribute the bread of life to the growing number of native-born Latinos in the United States. In the process I have also become familiar with creative proposals to meet the challenges facing the diverse Hispanic communities in the United States. This book seeks to better inform the Hispanic church of one particular set of challenges and the proposals being advanced to meet them.

A GENERATION THAT MUST NOT BE OVERLOOKED

Recent Pew Hispanic Center[10] tabulations of the 2009 American Community Survey[11] found that 62 percent of all Latinos are native-born, that is, they were born in the United States.[12] Predictably, another important study revealed that 61 percent of all native-born Latinos were English-dominant, 35 percent were bilingual, while only 4 percent indicated that they were Spanish-dominant.[13] These findings were similar to those published in 2005 by a multicultural market research firm that found that English is the undisputed language of preference among 1.5 generation[14] and second-generation Latinos and becomes

---

[10]The Pew Hispanic Center is a project of the Pew Research Center, a nonpartisan "fact tank" that provides information on the issues, attitudes and trends shaping America and the world. It is supported by the Pew Charitable Trusts. More information is available at <http://pewhispanic.org/>.

[11]The American Community Survey (ACS) is an ongoing statistical survey by the U. S. Census Bureau. The ACS is the largest household survey in the U.S., with a sample of about 3 million addresses per year providing estimates of the size and characteristics of the resident populations. More information is available at <www.census.gov/acs/www/>.

[12]Pew Hispanic Center, "Statistical Portrait of Hispanics in the United States, 2009" (Washington, D.C.: Pew Hispanic Center, February 17, 2011), Table 2.

[13]Pew Hispanic Center and Kaiser Family Foundation, "2002 National Survey of Latinos" (Washington, D.C.: Pew Hispanic Center, December 2002), p. 45.

[14]The term *1.5 generation* refers to people who immigrate to a new country before their early teens.

nearly absolute among third-generation Latinos.[15]

Here is the problem. Conventional Spanish-speaking ministry models are unintentionally designed to preserve the language and cultural preferences of foreign-born Latinos. Sadly, this is usually done at the expense of their native-born English-dominant children and grandchildren. Though they represent more than 60 percent of all Latinos in this country, native-born Latinos, especially those who are English dominant, have been largely ignored by denominational and local church leaders who uncritically equate "Hispanic ministry" with "Spanish-language ministry."

The primary assumption underlying this study is that the unique social and cultural context of U.S-born Latinos of Cuban, Mexican and Puerto Rican ancestry calls upon church leaders to prayerfully and thoughtfully reexamine the viability of their traditional approaches to ministry.[16] Like the Greek-speaking Jews described in Acts 6:1-4, "Hellenized Latinos" (i.e., English-dominant Latinos) are going overlooked, at least in so far as most Hispanic Protestant, evangelical and Pentecostal churches are concerned. The present study addresses this problem, highlighting and analyzing the efforts of dozens of churches across the United States that are successfully reaching all Latinos, including native-born English-dominant Latinos. Given the diversity of the Hispanic population in the United States—our many countries of origin, and cultural and even linguistic differences—it is difficult for one book to be all-encompassing of the religious experiences of Latinos in the United States. Since my primary interest is in ministries that are having success reaching U.S.-born Latinos, it made sense to focus attention on major urban centers with the largest and oldest Hispanic populations. Therefore churches highlighted in this study are found in major urban centers including Chicago, Dallas/Fort Worth, Los An-

---

[15]New American Dimensions, "Made in America: Communicating with Young Latinos," accessed on Nov. 8, 2008 <www.newamericandimensions.com/downloads/NADAcculturation Study.pdf>.

[16]The churches highlighted in this study primarily target Latinos of Mexican, Cuban and Puerto Rican ancestry. Together these three subgroups represent 78 percent of the Hispanic population in the United States. See the U.S. Census Bureau, Population Division, Ethnic & Hispanic Statistics Branch, "The Hispanic Population in the United States: 2008" (Washington, D.C.: U.S. Census Bureau, March 2008), Table 2.

geles, Miami, New York and San Antonio. The choice of these major urban centers made sense for another reason. These cities also have heavy concentrations of Latinos of Cuban, Mexican and Puerto Rican ancestry, the three largest Hispanic subgroups. Observations and personal interviews with leaders at dozens of churches in cities across the country with the largest and oldest Hispanic populations reveal that the hegemony of the Spanish-speaking immigrant-church model is being challenged by a growing number of multilingual, multigenerational Hispanic churches that effectively reach U.S.-born English-dominant Latinos.[17]

BACK TO EGYPT: AN AUTOBIOGRAPHICAL NOTE

This study was birthed from a personal journey to rediscover my own ethnic roots, roots that were partially lost during an acculturation and assimilation process that extended over three generations. With few reservations this process was reinforced by my grandparents, parents, teachers and ancestral church. Along with many other upwardly mobile Mexican-Americans born and raised in *el norte* (the United States), I gradually lost touch with many of my historical and cultural roots.

Like many other native-born Latino Christians my spiritual pilgrimage resembled that of Moses. On the one hand, like Moses, I was raised and educated as an Egyptian (i.e., Anglo) in order to live and succeed in Egypt (i.e., the United States). As a consequence of not speaking Spanish and not having an adequate appreciation for the idiosyncrasies of my ancestral culture and homeland, I too was rejected by the Hebrews (i.e., foreign-born *mexicanos*) who contemptuously referred to me as a *pocho* or *agringado,* an anglicized Mexican. On the other hand, like Moses, I also discovered that due to my surname, dark complexion, socioeconomic status and affinity for things *mexicano* I was still considered too Mexican to be completely welcomed within mainstream North American society. Virgilio Elizondo

[17]This research model has been successfully used by those who study African American urban churches as well as by those who study contemporary urban ministry paradigms across the United States. See Nile Harper, *Urban Churches, Vital Signs: Beyond Charity Toward Justice* (Grand Rapids: Eerdmans, 1999), and Ronald J. Sider, Philip Olsson and Heidi Rolland Unruh, *Churches That Make a Difference* (Grand Rapids: Baker, 2002).

describes the unenviable position of many native-born Latinos like me who are "part of and despised by both" parent cultures.[18] Like millions of U.S.-born Latinos, I was forced to live "in the hyphen" between Mexican and American.

Then, like Moses, I received a call from the Lord to return to my people in the barrio with the gospel of Jesus Christ. There was only one problem: three generations of acculturation and assimilation separated me from the majority of poorly educated, working-class Latinos living in underserved at-risk urban barrios on the periphery of U.S. society. Therefore, after I received the "proper" theological training, the Lord led me to Puebla, Mexico, where I became fluent in Spanish while working for nine years in church planting and leadership development with *las iglesias de Cristo* (i.e., non-instrumental Churches of Christ). This experience allowed me to rediscover and appreciate my ancestral heritage as well as the sociohistorical and spiritual legacy of my people. Upon returning to Southern California in 1994, I accepted a position at Pepperdine University while completing a Ph.D. in intercultural studies (i.e., missiology) at Fuller Theological Seminary in Pasadena, California.

AN OVERVIEW OF THE BOOK

In order to understand the relevance of the case studies presented in this study, readers must understand the sociohistorical and cultural context of U.S.-born Latinos. Therefore, in chapter one I will provide a careful analysis of the available demographic, historical and sociological data needed to comprehend the social and cultural distance that exists between foreign-born and U.S.-born Latinos. I will also indentify important factors that contribute to and reinforce Hispanic ethnic identity and loyalty even among native-born Latinos with high levels of acculturation. Important and often overlooked factors include the legacy and effects of perceived discrimination and cultural conflict, which help explain the hesitancy of native-born Latinos to embrace churches of the dominant group. In other words, I will describe and analyze the

---

[18]Virgilio P. Elizondo, *Galilean Journey: The Mexican-American Promise* (Maryknoll, N.Y.: Orbis, 2000), p. 53.

dilemma of "living in the hyphen" between Latin-American and Anglo-American cultures. Observations at the target churches and interviews with Hispanic church leaders will illustrate the findings cited in the pertinent demographic, historical and sociological research.

Chapter two explores how linguistic, cultural and socioeconomic factors have reshaped ministry paradigms and practices in churches that traditionally targeted foreign-born Spanish-dominant Latinos but now *also* successfully target U.S.-born English-dominant Latinos. The remarkable success of these multilingual, multigenerational Hispanic churches reveals that a commitment to serve, evangelize and disciple native-born Latinos obliges church leaders to embrace contextually appropriate ministry models for English-dominant Latinos. These new ministry models are attracting U.S.-born Latinos who often feel out of place or even unwelcome in churches that are exclusively Spanish speaking, but who due to socioeconomic and cultural differences are also reluctant to assimilate into churches of the dominant group (i.e., non-Hispanic whites). Objections and obstacles faced by these pioneering pastors and churches will also be examined.

Chapter three will include an introduction to the context, history, principles and practices of English-speaking Hispanic evangelical churches born in the barrio. These churches have historically and primarily attracted native-born English-dominant Latinos. However, in an effort to embrace the non-Hispanic spouses, family members and friends of their members, these churches prefer to describe themselves as "multiethnic, predominantly Hispanic churches." Included in this chapter are descriptions and analysis of three church-planting movements that successfully target at-risk English-dominant Latinos across the United States. The descriptions and analysis of churches highlighted in chapter three and four will be based on official church histories, church websites and on-site observations, as well as personal interviews with movement founders, local pastors and lay leaders.[19]

The majority of the churches highlighted in this study combine their commitment to the Great Commission with an equally strong commit-

---

[19]Contact information for each church is listed in appendix A.

ment to compassion ministries and social justice, evident in many social services offered to their respective communities. Chapter four will feature and analyze the creative and holistic ministries that help these Hispanic congregations engage at-risk and underserved children, youth and families with good news and good works.

One of the outstanding characteristics of the churches targeted in this study is the ability of the pastoral staff to identify, train and empower indigenous leaders in the context of the local church. Contextually appropriate models of leadership development successfully shortcut traditional approaches that require aspiring pastors to attend a Bible college, Christian university or seminary for theological and ministerial training. Chapter five will highlight and analyze indefinitely reproducible approaches to leadership development in churches that are successfully reaching U.S.-born English-dominant Latinos in at-risk underserved communities.

The study concludes by identifying several challenges that face church leaders who desire to successfully target U.S.-born English-dominant Latinos in the twenty-first century. One of the greatest challenges is the need to recognize that the church's mission is to preach the gospel to all people. It is not to preserve the language and cultural preferences of any generation, whether foreign or native born. In the face of these "new Hispanic challenges," I will provide examples of vision, courage and sacrifice on the part of Hispanic church leaders who are meeting these challenges head on, recognizing the ever-changing face of Hispanic ministry in the United States.

KEY TERMS AND CONCEPTS DEFINED

In order to facilitate the reading of this book, definitions of key terms and concepts are provided below. The use of these terms and concepts is ubiquitous today, yet there is no consensus among scholars and practitioners regarding their meaning and utility in common parlance. Some of the following terms are used extensively in this study. Others inform my fundamental assumptions. So it is incumbent upon me to briefly address my understanding and use of each term and concept at the outset of the book.

***Hispanic* or *Latino/a*.** These terms will be used interchangeably to refer to all individuals of Latin American ancestry or with ties to the Spanish-speaking world who reside either legally or illegally within the borders of the United States of America. Generally, *Latino* will be used as a noun (e.g., native-born *Latinos*) and *Hispanic* will be used as an adjective (e.g., *Hispanic* churches).

Experts remind us that there is no single Hispanic ethnic population. However, all Hispanics in the United States compose the Hispanic population. We must also remember that the term *Hispanic* is a term developed and used uniquely in the United States. David Maldonado reminds us that "there are no Hispanics in Latin America! Mexicans, Puerto Ricans, or Salvadorans, along with other populations from Latin American nations, are defined as Hispanic when in the United States."[20]

***Hispanic*.** This term is not new. It can be traced back to the sixteenth century. But thanks to its use by the U.S. Census Bureau, it emerged in the middle and late 1970s to describe people from different backgrounds but sharing a common language and cultural heritage. It effectively served as a sociopolitical construct with relevance within the helping professions. By the late 1970s and early 1980s the term was being used regularly in the popular media. Commercially, the term was used to help market goods and services to Latinos. The use of *Hispanic* by the U.S. Census Bureau in the 1980 and 1990 censuses resulted in a creation of data that further reinforced the use of the term. This was especially true with regard to policies and programs targeting Latinos through public and private grants and other funding mechanisms.[21]

***Latino/a*.** Although the terms *Hispanic* and *Latino/a* are now commonly used interchangeably as in this study, the use of the term *Latino/a* can be traced to the early 1990s as a label used within the group as opposed to *Hispanic* used outside the group.[22] When describing them-

---

[20]David Maldonado Jr., ed., *Protestantes/Protestants: Hispanic Christianity Within Mainline Traditions* (Nashville: Abingdon, 1999), p. 12.

[21]Melvin Delgado, *Social Work with Latinos: A Cultural Assets Paradigm* (Oxford: Oxford University Press, 2007), p. 12. Delgado also notes that as a result of intergroup marriage, Latino identities related to countries of origin have blurred (ibid.).

[22]Ibid.

selves many of our people prefer the term *Latino/a* because it evokes their more recent cultural ties to Latin America in addition to their historic cultural roots in Spain.[23]

It should be noted that because their sense of ethnic identity is tied to their country of origin many people object to the labels *Hispanic* or *Latino/a*. For example, some Latinos of Mexican ancestry will say, "I'm Mexican, not Hispanic!"[24] This sentiment is shared by the vast majority of people of Latin American ancestry in the United States, both foreign born and native born.[25] It also reflects the opinion of many scholars who insist that there is no such thing as "Hispanic culture" or "Latino culture"—"only a collection of many national and regional cultures that happened to share language as a common element."[26] Jorge J. E. Garcia expresses even stronger reservations against the use of *Hispanic* or *Latino/a*. "There is nothing that so-called Hispanics/Latinos have in common. There is no unity, no reality which stands behind the name, for there are no common properties to all Hispanics/Latinos."[27]

Experts remind us that any prolonged debate over which term should be used is self-defeating because both terms ultimately fail to deal with the complexity of Hispanic existence in the United States.[28] This leads others to conclude that the vast differences in our countries of origin and cultural backgrounds will continue to inhibit the creation of a monolithic Hispanic or Latino identity.[29] Instead, we see ourselves as a "heterogeneous and complex" minority. Diversity is our trademark.[30]

Identification with the pan-ethnic terms *Hispanic* and *Latino/a* var-

---

[23]Ken Johnson-Mondragón, ed., *Pathways for Hope and Faith Among Hispanic Teens: Pastoral Reflections and Strategies Inspired by the National Study of Youth and Religion* (Stockton, Calif.: Instituto Fe y Vida, 2007), p. 6.

[24]Delgado, *Social Work with Latinos*, p. 16.

[25]Pew Hispanic Center and Kaiser Family Foundation, "2002 National Survey of Latinos," p. 24.

[26]Johnson-Mondragón, *Pathways for Hope and Faith*, p. 5.

[27]Jorge J. E. Garcia, *Hispanic/Latino Identity: A Philosophical Perspective* (Malden, Mass.: Blackwell, 2000), p. 21.

[28]Miguel A. De La Torre and Edwin David Aponte, *Introducing Latino/a Theologies* (Maryknoll, N.Y.: Orbis, 2001), p. 16.

[29]Ed Morales, *Living in Spanglish: The Search for Latino Identity in America* (New York: St. Martin's Press, 2002), p. 10.

[30]Ilan Stavans, *The Hispanic Condition: The Power of a People* (New York: HarperCollins, 2001), pp. 204, 31.

ies from person to person and may be driven by proximity to other national origin groups, as well as efforts to reinforce political awareness and interest.[31] In this regard *Hispanic* and *Latino/a* are helpful terms used to define the unity of various communities in the United States that have ties to Latin America or with the Spanish-speaking world. This is clearly the case with such religiously affiliated organizations as the National Hispanic Association of Evangelicals and the Academy of Catholic Hispanic Theologians of the United States, as well as publications such as the *Journal of Hispanic/Latino Theology* and *Apuntes: Theological Reflections from the Hispanic Margin*. Juan Martínez reminds us that *Hispanic* and *Latino/a* serve as useful umbrella terms that focus on what unites us. But he also reminds us that these terms also mask a whole series of differences among those called Latinos. Therefore, he insists that ministry among Latinos must take place "in the space between the unity and the multiple differences among our people."[32]

Evangelical(s). As in the case with *Hispanic* and *Latino/a*, there is no consensus regarding a precise definition of *evangelical*. But in his study of evangelicalism, William R. Baker has observed three distinctive traits that are consistently pointed out by experts: evangelicals maintain a commitment to the authority of the Bible, a zeal for evangelism and a belief in the need for regeneration through personal faith in Jesus Christ.[33] These are apparent in the definition of "evangelical" offered by James D. Hunter in *American Evangelicalism: Conservative Religion and the Quandary of Modernity*. "At the doctrinal core, contemporary evangelicals can be identified by their adherence to (1) the belief that the Bible is the inerrant Word of God, (2) the belief in the divinity of Christ, and (3) the belief in the efficacy of Christ's life, death, and physical resurrection for the salvation of the human soul."[34] My own

---

[31]Luis Ricardo Fraga, John A. Garcia, Rodney E. Hero, Michael Jones-Correa, Valerie Martínez-Ebers and Gary M. Segura, *Latino Lives in America: Making It Home* (Philadelphia: Temple University Press, 2010), p. 11.

[32]Juan Francisco Martínez, *Walk with the People: Latino Ministry in the United States* (Nashville: Abingdon, 2008), p. 16.

[33]William R. Baker, *Evangelicalism & the Stone-Campbell Movement* (Downers Grove, Ill.: InterVarsity Press, 2002), pp. 37-38.

[34]James D. Hunter, *American Evangelicalism: Conservative Religion and the Quandary of Modernity* (New Brunswick, N.J.: Rutgers University Press, 1983), p. 7.

understanding of *evangelical(s)* is informed by *The Oxford Dictionary of World Religions*, which suggests that this term usually refers to those Protestant Christians who stress belief in personal conversion and salvation by faith in the atoning death of Christ (usually termed "new birth" or "conversion"), belief in the Bible as the sole authority in matters of faith, and the importance of evangelism.[35]

Evangélico. Many readers may uncritically assume that *evangélico* is the Spanish equivalent of "evangelical." This is a common misunderstanding. In common parlance among Latin Americans and Spanish-dominant Latinos in the United States, *evangélico* is a term that is usually synonymous with the broader term "Protestant." Experts observe that since *evangelical* defines a specific religious movement in the United States, its meaning is much more limited than the traditional use of *evangélico* in Spanish. However, in the United States many Latinos are now using *evangélico* in a more limited sense where it is synonymous with evangelical.[36]

The gospel. In his provocative and prophetic book *The Church and Its Mission: A Shattering Critique from the Third World*, the late Orlando E. Costas reminds Latinos and others that *the gospel* is the fulfillment of the Old Testament messianic hope. It is the good news that God, through the death, burial and resurrection of his only begotten Son, freely offers renewal by the Holy Spirit and reconciliation with himself to all who approach him by placing their faith in and surrendering control of their lives to Jesus Christ as both Savior and Lord.[37]

As a member of the U.S. delegation at the Third Lausanne Congress on World Evangelization held in Cape Town, South Africa, in October 2010, I affirm with evangelicals from around the world that Jesus Christ of Nazareth stands at the center of the gospel, which responds to a fallen humanity "having no hope and without God in the world" (Eph 2:12). This was stated clearly in the Lausanne Covenant, a document influenced by well-recognized and respected Latin American and

---

[35]John Bowker, ed., *The Oxford Dictionary of World Religions* (New York: Oxford University Press, 1997), p. 326.

[36]Martínez, *Walk with the People*, p. 46.

[37]Orlando E. Costas, *The Church and Its Mission: A Shattering Critique from the Third World* (Wheaton, Ill.: Tyndale House, 1974), p. 64.

Hispanic evangelical church leaders including C. René Padilla, Orlando E. Costas, Juan Carlos Ortiz, Samuel Escobar, Luis Palau and Emilio A. Nuñez, among others.

> There is no other name by which we must be saved. All men and women are perishing because of sin, but God loves everyone, not wishing that any should perish but that all should repent. Yet those who reject Christ repudiate the joy of salvation and condemn themselves to eternal separation from God. To proclaim Jesus as "the Saviour of the world" is not to affirm that all people are either automatically or ultimately saved, still less to affirm that all religions offer salvation in Christ. Rather it is to proclaim God's love for a world of sinners and to invite everyone to respond to him as Saviour and Lord in the wholehearted personal commitment of repentance and faith.[38]

Therefore, along with evangelicals from around the world, I reject as false gospels those which deny human sin, divine judgment, the deity and incarnation of Jesus Christ, and the necessity of the cross and resurrection.[39]

At the Second Lausanne Congress on World Evangelization held in Manila, Philippines, in July 1989, delegates elaborated on the statement above from the "Lausanne Covenant." Similar to the pastors and churches highlighted in this study, they sought to draw attention to the "holistic nature" of the gospel.

> The gospel is the good news of God's salvation from the power of evil, the establishment of his eternal kingdom and his final victory over everything which defies his purpose. In his love God purposed to do this before the world began and effected his liberating plan over sin, death and judgment through the death of our Lord Jesus Christ.[40]

Thus the broader definition of the gospel assumed in this book would include but not be limited to the good news of Jesus Christ and

---

[38]The Lausanne Movement, "The Lausanne Covenant, Paragraph 3, 'The Uniqueness and Universality of Christ,'" in *Making Christ Known: Historic Mission Documents from the Lausanne Movement, 1974-1989,* ed. John Stott (Grand Rapids: Eerdmans, 1996), p. 16.

[39]The Lausanne Movement, "The Manila Manifesto, Paragraph A, 'The Whole Gospel,'" in *Making Christ Known: Historic Mission Documents from the Lausanne Movement, 1974-1989,* ed. John Stott (Grand Rapids: Eerdmans, 1996), p. 233.

[40]Ibid.

the salvation that God has provided through him. Yet it reaches beyond the mere proclamation of the Scriptures (e.g., 1 Cor 15:1-4) and the certainty of eternal life. The gospel includes the presence of the risen Lord as the object of the worship of the church. It includes the praxis of the church in its proclamation of the good news, including a Christ-like commitment to justice and mercy. The gospel also includes the Spirit of the risen Lord guiding his church as it lives out its missionary calling in every sociohistorical context. Finally, the gospel includes the prophetic Spirit of Christ challenging every culture as well as every church to submit to him as Lord as well as Savior.[41]

What then is *evangelism?* I endorse the definition from the Lausanne Covenant because it emphasizes that reconciliation to God lies at the very heart of the gospel.

> To evangelize is to spread the Good News that Jesus Christ died for our sins and was raised from the dead according to the Scriptures, and that as the reigning Lord he now offers the forgiveness of sins and the liberating gift of the Spirit to all who repent and believe. . . . [It] is the proclamation of the historical, biblical Christ as Saviour and Lord, with a view to persuading people to come to him personally and so be reconciled to God. . . . The results of evangelism include obedience to Christ, incorporation into his church and responsible service in the world.[42]

In chapter four it will become clear that I believe that the proclamation of the gospel and good works (including relief, development and structural change) are inseparable. Nevertheless, I will insist that for theological and logical reasons *evangelism is primary.*

Culture, enculturation* and *acculturation. The late Paul Heibert, distinguished professor of mission and anthropology at Trinity Evangelical Divinity School, defined culture succinctly as "the integrated system of learned patterns of behavior, ideas, and products characteristic of a society."[43] Critical to this brief definition offered by Heibert is

---

[41]Robert J. Schreiter, *Constructing Local Theologies* (Maryknoll, N.Y.: Orbis, 1985), p. 20.

[42]The Lausanne Movement, "The Lausanne Covenant, Paragraph 4, 'The Nature of Evangelism,'" in *Making Christ Known: Historic Mission Documents from the Lausanne Movement, 1974–1989,* ed. John Stott (Grand Rapids: Eerdmans, 1996), p. 20.

[43]Paul G. Heibert, *Cultural Anthropology* (Grand Rapids: Baker, 1983), p. 25.

the idea that culture is "learned." Gailyn Van Rheenen observes that culture is composed of five elements: *ideas*, mental images through which people perceive reality; *values*, the worth, importance and ethical input of ideas; *behavior*, the observable ways of doing things in culture; *products* or artifacts that make up visible, material culture; and *institutions*, the organizational structure of a culture. He reminds us that culture is always created within a specific *society*, that is, within a group of people "who use the customs of a culture and hold to its beliefs."[44]

Enculturation is the term used to describe the process by which children through observation, imitation and instruction by family and peers learn to become functioning members of their own society. *Acculturation* describes the process by which adults acquire the cultural competence to become functioning participants of a new or host culture. In other words, "acculturation is for adults what enculturation is for children."[45] Thus a child born to Mexican parents in Puebla is gradually *enculturated* into Mexican culture. Twenty years later when that child is an adult and chooses to migrate to Los Angeles, he may choose to become *acculturated* into mainstream American (i.e., Anglo) culture. In other words, an inquiry into a Latino's level of acculturation to the majority culture essentially asks, "To what extent is the person like an Anglo-American?"[46]

But how is culture learned? For a child born in Mexico, most people would say that learning Spanish is critical to successful *enculturation*. Later as an immigrant in the United States, most people would say that learning English is critical to successful *acculturation*. While no one dismisses the importance of language to learning one's own or a host culture, many overestimate the importance of language in the enculturation or acculturation process. This is often the case with first-generation Hispanic parents who are concerned that their English-dominant second-generation children will lose their culture if they "forget" or "lose" their Spanish. More often the fear is of losing the

---

[44]Gailyn Van Rheenen, *Missions: Biblical Foundations and Contemporary Strategies* (Grand Rapids: Zondervan, 1996), p. 81.

[45]Ibid., p. 85.

[46]Charles Negy and Donald J. Woods, "The Importance of Acculturation in Understanding Research with Hispanic-Americans," *Hispanic Journal of Behavioral Sciences* 14 (1992): 224.

intimacy that is shared in language, *en español*. But as Richard Rodríguez painfully reminds us, "intimacy is not trapped within words."[47]

In *The Silent Language*, Edward Hall maintains that language is just one of ten "primary message systems" found in every culture. Other message systems include values, beliefs and behaviors associated with such things as (1) time, (2) space and property, (3) methods of controlling others, including the use and sharing of resources, (4) family, kin and community, (5) work and the division of labor, (6) gender appropriate modes of speech, dress and conduct, (7) learning and instruction, (8) games, humor and play, and (9) conflict resolution including health procedures and beliefs.[48] While knowing or learning the language of a society is critical, language by itself does not convey everything one needs to know about a society's culture. This suggests that Latinos who do not speak Spanish or who speak it poorly can nonetheless become enculturated or acculturated into a Hispanic culture by means of the other nine primary message systems.[49]

***Cultural validity* and *cultural relativity*.** Missiologists speak of *cultural validity* or *cultural relativity* to refer to an anthropological perspective that assumes that all cultures are essentially equal to one another and therefore should not be quickly judged by outsiders. The terms imply that every culture must be evaluated according to its own standards, not according to those of another society. Thus an Anglo American missionary in Honduras or a foreign-born Cuban evangelist in Tampa, Florida, should never imply that his or her culture is superior to that of others. Instead, the definition of culture provided here assumes that all cultures are created by humans. Therefore all cultures have inherent strengths and weaknesses. "All cultures demonstrate satanic brokenness on the one hand and godly influences on the other. Cultures exhibit both a proclivity to sin, which alienates them from God, and attributes of goodness, reflecting divine presence."[50] While all cul-

---

[47]Richard Rodríguez, *Hunger of Memory: The Education of Richard Rodríguez* (New York: Bantam, 1982), p. 40.

[48]Edward Hall, *The Silent Language* (Garden City, N.Y.: Doubleday, 1973), pp. 38-59.

[49]Sherwood Lingenfelter, *Ministering Cross-Culturally: An Incarnational Model for Personal Relationships*, 2nd ed. (Grand Rapids: Baker Academic, 2003), p. 28.

[50]Van Rheenen, *Missions*, p. 82.

tures reflect a natural knowledge of God (Rom 1:18-21; 2:14-15), all cultures, including Anglo American and Hispanic cultures (plural) are contaminated by sinful human beings.

All cultures are what Sherwood Lingenfelter calls "palaces" and "prisons of disobedience." They are "palaces" because they provide human beings with "comfort, security, meaning and relationships." But they are also "prisons of disobedience" because they restrict our freedom to live the abundant life we were created for, the life provided for by Jesus Christ (Jn 10:10). Instead, every culture sets barriers between people, God and others. As such, every culture is judged by God.[51] This rejection and rebellion against God is often manifest in what we call "religion" (cf. Rom 1:18-23). Consequently, in word and deed Jesus challenged the traditional ideas, behavior, products and institutions of his society and culture. This is obvious not only in the Sermon on the Mount (Mt 5–7) but also in his critique of the teaching, behavior and institutions of the religious leaders of his day (Mt 15:1-20; 21:33-46; 23:1-36). Ultimately, it cost him his life. The same is true of many believers who took the gospel from Jerusalem to the ends of the earth (Acts 1:8). Implied in the message that Jesus is Lord and Savior and the only mediator between God and humanity (Jn 14:1-7; Acts 4:8-12; 1 Tim 2:3-7) is a critique of every culture, including Anglo American and Hispanic cultures, as a "prison of disobedience."

Similarly, Lesslie Newbigin observes that the New Testament repeatedly insists that "the revelation of God in Jesus Christ, with its burning center in the agony and death of Calvary, compels me to acknowledge that this world which God made and loves is in a state of alienation, rejection, and rebellion against him."[52] Thus the fundamental worldview assumptions, values, behaviors and institutions of human cultures are consistently judged by God. For example, Jews were persuaded to repent and turn to God in faith by recognizing the sovereign rule of Jesus Christ as Lord (Acts 2:36-41; 3:17-26; 4:8-12; 7:51-53; 13:16-31; 17:1-5). Devotees of the Roman gods Zeus and Hermes were

---

[51]Sherwood Lingenfelter, *Transforming Culture: A Challenge for Christian Mission*, 2nd ed. (Grand Rapids: Baker Academic, 2004), p. 20.
[52]Lesslie Newbigin, *The Gospel in a Pluralistic Society* (Grand Rapids: Eerdmans, 1989), p. 175.

told to "turn from these worthless things to the living God" (Acts 14:15). Devotees of the gods of the Greek Pantheon in Athens were sensitively yet boldly informed that their religious assumptions and practices stemmed from "ignorance" of the divine will and were urged to repent (Acts 17:22-31). In Ephesus, those who believed the gospel of Jesus Christ publicly burned valuable sacred texts associated with their former religious practices (Acts 19:17-21). Devotees of the goddess "Artemis of the Ephesians" were threatened because Paul was persuading the multitudes that manmade gods are not gods at all, thus "depriving" Artemis of her divine majesty (Acts 19:23-27). And the author of 1 Peter reminds his readers that "you were ransomed from the futile ways inherited from your ancestors . . . with the precious blood of Christ" (1 Pet 1:18-19).

As God's missionary people, we have been sent into the world just as Jesus Christ was sent into the world by the Father (Jn 20:21)—in our case, as disciples of Jesus among Latinos and others in and beyond our communities in the United States. Consequently, we must not allow our ethnocentrism to blind us to the prisons of disobedience evident in every culture, including our own.[53] Instead, we must embrace our call as pilgrims, *peregrinos*, those Peter refers to as living in "exile" in their homeland (1 Pet 1:17). Whether it is in a *finca* in El Salvador or a suburb of Dallas, we too are "aliens and exiles" whose ultimate allegiance is not to "our people" (*nuestra raza* or *nuestro pueblo*) nor is it to the United States of America. Our allegiance is to Jesus Christ! Therefore as disciples of Christ we are all *paisanos* (fellow countrymen) of a *patria* (homeland) that is not of this world (Phil 3:20; Heb 11:13-16).

BECOMING ALL THINGS TO ALL LATINOS

In his seminal study *The Hispanic Challenge: Opportunities Confronting the Church* (1993), Manuel Ortiz correctly observes that so long as legal and illegal immigration from Latin America and the Caribbean contin-

---

[53]The so-called low view of culture proposed here stands in contrast with that of others who argue for a so-called high or neutral view of culture. See Charles H. Kraft, *Christianity and Culture* (Maryknoll, N.Y.: Orbis, 1981) and Marvin K. Mayers, *Christianity Confronts Culture* (Grand Rapids: Zondervan, 1987).

ues to the United States there will be a need for Spanish-speaking immigrant churches. But it is time for church and denominational leaders to recognize that like the Hellenized Jews mentioned in Acts 6:1, many of the U.S.-born children and grandchildren of the immigrant generation are going overlooked in the daily distribution of bread in Hispanic churches "that perpetuate the culture of the first generation."[54]

As this study will demonstrate, native-born Latinos find themselves "living in the hyphen." While we often feel rejected by the foreign-born for being *agringado* (Americanized), we also perceive that we are treated as second-class citizens in the country of our birth and often treated as "outsiders" in the churches of the dominant group. Virgilio Elizondo, one of the most influential Latino theologians of the past twenty-five years, has summarized our predicament: "We have always been treated as foreigners in our own countryside—exiles who never left home."[55]

This study is aimed at drawing long-overdue attention to emerging Hispanic leaders and churches who are meeting the "challenges" outlined by Ortiz in 1993. This new generation of Hispanic leaders is dedicated to becoming all things to all Latinos—including the silent majority who are native born and English dominant, "living in the hyphen" between Latin-American and Anglo-American cultures. Humbly and prayerfully I commend this study, particularly the examples of faithful and courageous pastors and churches highlighted herein, to all those passionate about sharing the gospel of Jesus Christ among *all* Latinos in the United States.

---

[54]Manuel Ortiz, *The Hispanic Challenge: Opportunities Confronting the Church* (Downers Grove, Ill.: InterVarsity Press, 1993), p. 39.

[55]Virgilio P. Elizondo, "Mestizaje as a Locus of Theological Reflection," in *Mestizo Christianity: Theology from a Latino Perspective*, ed. Arturo J. Bañuelas (Maryknoll, N.Y.: Orbis, 1995), p. 9.

~ 1 ~

LIVING IN THE HYPHEN

But by the grace of God I am what I am,
and his grace toward me has not been in vain.

1 CORINTHIANS 15:10

I gradually became more and more aware of the many things
that I was not: I was not and would never be, even if I wanted to,
a regular U.S.-American. Yet neither would I be a puro mexicano.

VIRGILIO ELIZONDO, *THE FUTURE IS MESTIZO*

IN ORDER TO UNDERSTAND THE RELEVANCE of the case studies presented in this book, readers must understand the socioeconomic and cultural context of U.S.-born Latinos. A careful analysis of the available demographic data will help church and denominational leaders better comprehend the social and cultural distance that exists between U.S.-born and foreign-born Latinos as well as between U.S.-born Latinos and members of the dominant group (i.e., Anglo Americans). With respect to the latter, I will also identify important factors that contribute to and reinforce Hispanic ethnic identity and loyalty even among native-born Latinos with high levels of assimilation and acculturation. Important and often overlooked factors include the legacy and effects of discrimination and intercultural conflict, which help explain the hesitancy of native-born Latinos to embrace churches of the dominant group. In other words, I will describe and analyze the dilemma of "living in the hyphen" between Latin-American and Anglo-American cultures. Observations at the target churches and interviews with Hispanic church leaders and members will illustrate the findings cited in the pertinent demographic and sociological research.

Just as many public and private agencies utilize demographic information to validate their policies and programs, the church, too, needs to familiarize itself with the unique socioeconomic context in which more than fifty million Latinos live. With a clearer understanding of the socioeconomic situation of Latinos, messengers of Christ may enhance their efforts to contextualize the gospel, incorporate greater numbers of Latinos meaningfully into the body of Christ, and prepare larger numbers of Latinos to participate actively and fruitfully in the mission of God.

POPULATION GROWTH AMONG LATINOS

During the past four decades the Hispanic population has experienced extraordinary growth. According to the U.S. Census Bureau, in 1970 the Hispanic population was 9.6 million, or 4.7 percent of the total population. In 2000 the Hispanic population had increased to 35.3 million, representing 12.5 percent of the total population.[1] The most recent Census Bureau figures reveal that in 2010 the Hispanic population reached 50.5 million, representing more than 16.3 percent of the U.S. population. Latinos, who can be of any race, are now the largest minority group in the United States.[2]

In the United States Latinos are a heterogeneous group comprising all those who trace their ancestry to the Spanish-speaking world, the Caribbean and Latin America (see table 1). Several distinct national origin subgroups are therefore included under the pan-ethnic terms *Hispanic* and *Latino* (see figure 1). In 2009, the U.S. Census Bureau indicated that the Mexican-descent population is by far the largest subgroup, constituting 65.5 percent of the total Hispanic population. Puerto Ricans (9.1%), Cubans (3.5%) and Dominicans (2.8%) consti-

---

[1]U.S. Census Bureau, 1970, 1980, 1990 and 2000 Decennial Censuses.

[2]Karen R. Humes, Nicholas A. Jones and Roberto R. Ramirez, "Overview of Race and Hispanic Origin: 2010," 2010 Census Briefs, C2020BR-02 (Washington, D.C.: U.S. Census Bureau, March 2011).

Table 1. Hispanic Origin by Type: 2000 and 2009

	2000	Percent	2009	Percent
Mexican	20,640,711	58.5	31,673,700	65.5
Puerto Rican	3,406,178	9.6	4,411,604	9.1
Cuban	1,241,685	3.5	1,677,158	3.5
Dominican	764,945	2.2	1,360,476	2.8
All Central American	1,686,937	4.8	4,140,186	8.7
All South American	1,353,562	3.8	2,831,255	5.9
Spaniard	100,135	0.3	613,585	1.3
All other Hispanic or Latino	6,111,665	17.3	1,640,180	3.4
Total	35,305,818	100	48,348,144	100

tute the next largest subgroups. All Central Americans and all South Americans account for 8.7 percent and 5.9 percent of the Hispanic population respectively. "Other Hispanic" (3.4%) includes all those who provided general Hispanic-origin responses such as "Hispanic," "Spanish" or "Latino."[3]

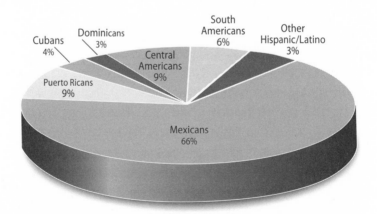

Figure 1. Hispanic population by subgroups

[3]Betsy Guzman, "The Hispanic Population," Census 2000 Brief, C2KBR/01-3 (Washington, D.C.: U.S. Census Bureau, May 2001), p. 2; Pew Hispanic Center, "Statistical Portrait of Hispanics in the United States, 2009" (Washington, D.C.: Pew Hispanic Center, February 2011), Table 6.

According to the 2010 Census, the population of the United States grew by 27.3 million people, or 9.7 percent, between 2000 and 2010. By contrast, the Hispanic population grew by 43 percent, rising from 35.3 million in 2000 to 50.5 million in 2010.[4] That is an increase of 15.2 million Latinos, which accounted for over half of the increase of the total population (see table 2). Experts at the U.S. Census Bureau and the Pew Hispanic Center are confident that the rapid growth of the Hispanic population in the United States will continue throughout the first half of the twenty-first century. Population projections indicate that from 2005 through 2050 the Hispanic population will account for the majority of the nation's population growth. Latinos are projected to make up 29 percent of the U.S. population in 2050, compared with 14 percent in 2005.[5]

Table 2. U.S. Population by Race and Ethnicity, 2000 and 2010 (in millions)

	2000	2010	Percent of Population	Change, 2000 to 2010
Total Population	281.4	308.8	100.0	9.7%
Hispanic	35.3	50.5	16.30	43.0
Non-Hispanic White alone	194.6	196.8	63.70	1.2
Non-Hispanic Black alone	33.9	37.7	12.20	12.3
Non-Hispanic Asian alone	10.1	14.5	4.70	43.3

Note: The three major racial groups include only non-Hispanics. People of Hispanic origin may be of any race.

Source: Pew Hispanic Center and 2010 Census Brief C2010BR-02 issued March 2011

HECHO (MADE) IN THE U.S.A.

In contrast with the 1980s and 1990s, when the majority of the new growth was attributed to legal and undocumented immigration, the Hispanic population growth in the first decade of the twenty-first century has been more a product of the natural increase of the existing population.[6] With native births outpacing immigration as the key source of growth, an important shift is taking place in the makeup of

---

[4]Humes, Jones and Ramirez, "Overview of Race and Hispanic Origin."

[5]Jeffrey S. Passel and D'Vera Cohn, "US Populations Projections 2005-2050" (Washington, D.C.: Pew Hispanic Center, February 2008), p. i.

[6]Richard Fry, "Latino Settlement in the New Century" (Washington, D.C.: Pew Hispanic Center, October 2008), p. i.

the Hispanic population in the United States. Table 3 reveals that in 2009 native-born Latinos accounted for 62.6 percent of the Hispanic population in the United States.[7]

Table 3. Nativity Among Latinos

	2008 Population	2009 Population	Percent 2008	Percent 2009
Native Born	28,985,169	30,278,868	61.9	62.6
Foreign Born	17,837,307	18,069,276	38.1	37.4
Total	46,822,476	48,348,144	100.0	100.0

Source: Pew Hispanic Center Tabulations of 2000 Census and 2009 ACS, Table 5

Significant differences exist between native-born and foreign-born Latinos in terms of median age, language use, education and income levels, and levels of assimilation and acculturation. These important differences have profound implications not only in the realm of public policy, but also in the realm of religion, especially for evangelical Christians.

Table 4 reveals that the Hispanic population is much younger than the rest of the U.S. population. For example, the average age of non-Hispanic whites in 2009 was forty-one, while the average age for Latinos was twenty-seven. The average age drops significantly when considering only the native born, who made up 61 percent of the Hispanic population.[8]

As a result of massive immigration from Latin America and the Caribbean in the 1980s and 1990s, Latinos now make up 22 percent of all children under the age of eighteen in the United States. That figure is up from 9 percent in 1980.[9] Of Latinos under the age of eighteen, nearly 90 percent are U.S. citizens by birth. In fact, the size of the second generation has quadrupled between 1980 and 2007.[10]

---

[7]Pew Hispanic Center, "Statistical Portrait of Hispanics in the United States, 2009," Table 5. These figures are almost identical to those reported in 2006. See Pew Hispanic Center, "A Statistical Portrait of Hispanics at Mid-Decade" (Washington, D.C.: Pew Hispanic Center, September 18, 2006), Table 2.

[8]Pew Hispanic Center, "Statistical Portrait of Hispanics in the United States, 2009," Table 9.

[9]Richard Fry and Jeffrey S. Passel, "Latino Children: A Majority Are U.S.-Born Offspring of Immigrants" (Washington, D.C.: Pew Hispanic Center, May 2009), p. 1.

[10]Ibid., p. 3.

Table 4. Median Age by Sex, Race and Ethnicity

	All	Male	Female
Hispanic	27	27	27
Native born	17	17	18
Foreign born	38	37	39
Non-Hispanic White	41	39	42
Non-Hispanic Black	32	30	34
Non-Hispanic Asian	36	35	37
Other non-Hispanics	23	22	24
All	36	35	38

Source: Pew Hispanic Center Tabulations of 2009 ACS, Table 9

LANGUAGE USAGE AMONG LATINOS

One of the most significant differences between foreign-born and U.S.-born Latinos concerns language use. In 2002 the Pew Hispanic Center and the Kaiser Family Foundation published the "2002 National Survey of Latinos," the most comprehensive survey of Hispanic attitudes and experiences, including language use. Their findings reveal that foreign-born Latinos are overwhelmingly "Spanish dominant," while U.S.-born Latinos are overwhelmingly "English dominant" (see table 5).[11]

More specifically, the 2002 National Survey of Latinos found that only 7 percent of second-generation Latinos were Spanish dominant, while 47 percent were bilingual and 46 percent were English dominant. Only 22 percent of third-generation Latinos reported being bilingual, while 78 percent reported that they predominantly spoke English.[12] A later study found that although many third- and later-generation Latinos know how to speak Spanish, they do not often do so.[13] Similar findings were reported in a study of U.S.-born Latino Roman Catholics:

---

[11]Pew Hispanic Center and Kaiser Family Foundation, "2002 National Survey of Latinos" (Washington, D.C.: Pew Hispanic Center, December 2002), p. 45.

[12]Ibid.

[13]Shirin Hakimzadeh and D'Vera Cohn, "English Usage Among Hispanics" (Washington, D.C.: Pew Hispanic Center, November 2007), pp. 4-5.

Table 5. Foreign/Native-Born Language Use

	Foreign-Born Latinos	**Native-Born Latinos**
English-dominant	4%	61%
Bilingual	24%	35%
Spanish-dominant	72%	4%

Source: Pew Hispanic Center 2002 National Survey of Latinos

For the great majority, their operative language is English. While they may speak Spanish at home, or at least understand their parents who speak to them in Spanish (though they respond in English), English is the language they use in school. It is the language of their music, their movies, and their radio. It is the language in which they communicate with their peers and friends. Because of their almost constant immersion in English outside of the family, their English vocabulary far outstrips in size and sophistication the Spanish vocabulary they use primarily to address domestic issues and tasks. In addition, for many, Spanish is an oral language. They can neither read nor write Spanish with any fluency.[14]

These observations contradict those of new nativists, including Samuel P. Huntington. In *Who Are We? Challenges to America's National Identity*, Huntington has argued that unlike earlier immigrant groups, Latinos' refusal to learn English and assimilate into American society is now threatening to split the United States into two nations, one English speaking and the other Spanish speaking.[15] It is important to note that Huntington is correct when he observes that Latinos are holding on to their ancestral language longer than earlier immigrant populations did.[16] However, those who have carefully examined the available U.S. Census figures and subsequent Pew Hispanic Center surveys con-

---

[14]Gary Riebe-Estrella, "A Youthful Community: Theological and Ministerial Challenges," *Theological Studies* 65 (2004): 314.

[15]Samuel P. Huntington, *Who Are We? The Challenges to America's National Identity* (New York: Simon and Schuster, 2004), pp. 316-24.

[16]Among earlier immigrant groups, foreign-language use usually becomes extinct by the third generation, when English proficiency becomes universal. See Alejandro Portes and Lingxin Hao, "E Pluribus Unum: Bilingualism and the Loss of Language in the Second Generation," *Sociology of Education* 71 (1998): 269-94.

clude that the data "reveal both a high degree of assimilation among American Hispanics, and no real difference between Hispanics and other [immigrant] groups in their ability to use English."[17] The most obvious difference in language use between earlier immigrant groups and Latinos is bilingualism, which persists among a greater percentage of second- and later-generation Latinos than it did among earlier immigrant groups.[18]

EDUCATIONAL ATTAINMENT AMONG LATINOS

Hispanic educational attainment levels are increasing. But they continue to be lower compared to non-Latinos. According to Pew Hispanic Center tabulations of the 2009 American Community Survey, 39 percent of Latinos twenty-five years of age and older do not have a high school diploma, compared to 9.6 percent of the white population, 14.6 percent of the Asian population and 18.4 percent of the black population.[19] Table 6 reveals comparisons between percentages of non-Latinos and Latinos at five different educational-attainment levels.

When considering educational attainment, it is important to differentiate between native-born Latinos and those who are foreign born. The tabulations provided by the Pew Hispanic Center (table 6) reveal that education-attainment levels differ noticeably between native-born and foreign-born Latinos and between Latinos and other racial and ethnic groups.

EMPLOYMENT, EARNINGS AND POVERTY AMONG LATINOS

As one might expect, better paying jobs that require higher education and trained skills often elude Latinos. A statistical portrait of Hispanics in 2008 revealed that compared to non-Hispanic whites most Lati-

---

[17]Dennis Brown, "English Spoken Here? What the 2000 Census Tells Us About Language in the USA," Department of English, University of Illinois, accessed October 10, 2009, p. 5 <www.english.illinois.edu/-people-/faculty/debaron/403/403readings/english%20spoken .pdf>.

[18]Pew Hispanic Center and Kaiser Family Foundation, "Bilingualism" (Washington, D.C.: Pew Hispanic Center, March 2004), p. 5.

[19]Pew Hispanic Center, "Statistical Portrait of Hispanics in the United States, 2009," Table 22.

Table 6. Educational Attainment of U.S. Population 25 Years and Over

	Less than 9th grade	9th to 12th Grade	H.S. Graduate	Some College	College Graduate	Total
Percent Distribution						
Hispanic	23.5	15.5	26.0	22.2	12.7	100.0
Native born	8.9	13.5	29.2	31.9	16.6	100.0
Foreign born	34.6	17.1	23.7	14.9	9.7	100.0
Non-Hispanic White	3.0	6.6	29.3	30.0	31.1	100.0
Non-Hispanic Black	5.4	13.0	31.6	32.3	17.7	100.0
Non-Hispanic Asian	8.6	6.0	16.0	19.6	49.9	100.0
Other non Hispanic	5.0	9.6	27.6	35.3	22.6	100.0
All	6.3	8.5	28.5	28.9	27.9	100.0

Source: Pew Hispanic Center Tabulations of 2009 ACS, Table 22

nos work in blue-collar jobs (table 7). In fact, only 5.0 percent of all Latinos sixteen years of age and older serve in managerial positions, compared to 10.2 percent of non-Hispanic whites, while 8.9 percent of Latinos work in building and grounds cleaning and maintenance compared with only 3.0 percent of non-Hispanic whites.[20]

However, figures vary significantly when nativity is taken into consideration. Interestingly, the 2002 National Survey of Latinos found that bilingual and English-dominant Latinos had significantly higher household incomes than those who are Spanish dominant (table 7). Predictably, bilingual and English-dominant Latinos are much more likely to work in white-collar jobs than Spanish-dominant Latinos.[21]

MARRIAGE PATTERNS AMONG LATINOS

Before moving on to discuss the importance and implications of ethnic identity, especially for U.S.-born Latinos, one additional difference between native-born and foreign-born Latinos is worth men-

---

[20]Ibid., Table 28.
[21]Pew Hispanic Center and Kaiser Family Foundation, "2002 National Survey of Latinos," p. 17.

Table 7. Earnings and Employment Among Latinos

Household Income	Foreign-Born Latinos	Native-born Latinos
Less than $30,000	57%	37%
$30,000-$50,000	20	28
$50,000+	11	27
Don't know	12	8
Occupation		
White Collar (Net)	31	69
Blue Collar (Net)	65	28
Other	3	3

Source: Pew Hispanic Center 2002 National Survey of Latinos, Table 1.11

tioning. Foreign-born Latinos, like immigrants in general, tend to marry within their ethnic or racial group. However, this is not true of native-born Latinos. According to a recent study published by the Pew Hispanic Center, 32 percent of second-generation and 57 percent of third-plus generation Latinos marry outside of their ethnic or racial group.[22]

These findings suggest that significant differences do in fact exist between native-born and foreign-born Latinos in terms of median age, language use, education levels, employment, income levels and marriage patterns. Scholars are convinced that these demographic differences reflect different levels of acculturation. What then are the factors that account for different levels of acculturation observed among Latinos?

FACTORS INFLUENCING LEVELS OF ACCULTURATION

Linguistic factors. Higher levels of acculturation have been positively correlated to several linguistic and socioeconomic factors. For example, a positive correlation has been found between fluency in English

---

[22]Robert Suro and Jeffrey S. Passel, "The Rise of the Second Generation: Changing Patterns in Hispanic Population Growth" (Washington, D.C.: Pew Hispanic Center, October 2003), p. 9.

and higher levels of acculturation. That is, greater fluency in English leads to higher levels of acculturation.[23] The evidence suggests that among native-born Latinos there is significant social pressure to convert to English dominance with a resulting decline in competence in Spanish and a rise in acculturation levels.[24] The data is compelling to support the claim of Richard Alba and his colleagues that the overwhelming majority of Latinos are speaking "only English by the third generation."[25]

Socioeconomic factors. Research has also revealed a positive relationship between acculturation levels and socioeconomic status, suggesting that the more acculturated Latinos come from backgrounds with higher standards of living and better educated parents.[26] Higher levels of acculturation are also positively related to increased family involvement with external social systems such as school, work, community and other institutions in the United States.[27] These findings confirm the claim made by Professor Daniel Sánchez that schooling, media and peers positively influence acculturation levels among the children and grandchildren of immigrants. Sánchez observes that the use of English as the primary language of instruction and socialization in public and private schools, and as the language used in the media preferred by children, adolescents and young adults, has an overall negative effect on Spanish

---

[23]Israel Cuellar, Bill Nyberg, Roberto Maldonado and Robert E. Roberts, "Ethnic Identity and Acculturation in a Young Adult Mexican-Origin Population," *Journal of Community Psychology* 25, no. 6 (1997): 535-49.

[24]Alejandro Portes and Ruben Rumbaut, *Legacies: The Story of the Immigrant Second Generation* (Berkeley: University of California Press, 2001).

[25]Richard Alba, John Logan, Amy Lutz and Brian Stults, "Only English by the Third Generation? Loss and Preservation of the Mother Tongue Among the Grandchildren of Contemporary Immigrants," *Demography* 39 (2002): 480.

[26]A positive correlation between acculturation and socioeconomic status was found in Charles Negy and Donald J. Woods, "A Note on the Relationship between Acculturation and Socioeconomic Status," *Hispanic Journal of Behavioral Sciences* 14 (1992): 248-51; David R. Moyerman and Bruce D. Forman, "Acculturation and Adjustment: A Meta-Analytic Study," *Hispanic Journal of Behavioral Sciences* 14 (1992): 163-200; and in Israel Cuéllar, Bill Arnold and Roberto Maldonado, "Acculturation Rating Scale for Mexican Americans-II: A Revision of the Original ARSMA Scale," *Hispanic Journal of Behavioral Sciences* 17 (1995): 257-304.

[27]Erich Rueschenberg and Raymond Buriel, "Mexican American Family Functioning and Acculturation: A Family Systems Perspective," *Hispanic Journal of Behavioral Sciences* 11 (1989): 232-42.

language retention, thereby increasing levels of acculturation.[28]

Interviews and observations at the churches highlighted in this study substantiate the findings in the research cited above. Native-born Latinos at the churches described in this book are overwhelmingly English dominant and manifest significantly higher levels of acculturation than their immigrant parents and grandparents.

A fundamental assumption of this study is that an appreciation for the important differences that exist between foreign-born and native-born Latinos in terms of projected population growth, median age, language use, education, employment, income levels and marriage patterns will have profound implications for those who desire to minister effectively among all Latinos. One obvious implication is that "one-size-fits-all" approaches to Hispanic ministry must be abandoned in favor of approaches that take seriously the socioeconomic and cultural differences that exist among Latinos in the United States, especially between foreign-born and native-born Latinos. For example, the primary language used in outreach, preaching, teaching and worship will be different depending on the target audience. Interviews with Mexican, Cuban and Puerto Rican pastors across the United States confirmed the obvious: foreign-born Latinos prefer ministries and programs conducted in Spanish, while second- and especially third-generation Latinos prefer ministries and programs in English. As we will see in chapter two, when churches recognized this significant difference and adjusted their programs and ministries accordingly, they experienced almost immediate success in terms of the numbers of U.S-born Latinos that responded to their contextually appropriate approaches.

If second- and particularly third-generation Latinos prefer English to Spanish, then some church and denominational leaders might ask, "Rather than create parallel ministries and programs in English for U.S.-born Latinos, why not 'mainstream' English-dominant Latinos into the programs and ministries of the dominant group?" As I will demonstrate below, a number of factors combine to create a cultural and socioeconomic barrier between many U.S.-born English-speaking Latinos and dominant-group churches.

---

[28]Daniel R. Sánchez, *Hispanic Realities Impacting America: Implications for Evangelism & Missions* (Fort Worth, Tex.: Church Starting Network, 2006), pp. 82-83.

WHO ARE WE?

¿De dónde eres? (Where are you from?) For Latinos in the United States, this question is usually less about geography and more about ethnic identity. Its actual meaning is closer to, "Who are you?" The 2002 National Survey of Latinos discovered that among all Latino adults eighteen years and older, the overwhelming majority preferred "to identify themselves by the country where they or their parents or ancestors were born." That is, they preferred to identify themselves as "Mexican," "Puerto Rican," "Cuban," and so on. While virtually all foreign-born Latinos (95%) preferred to identify themselves by their country of origin, a vast majority (74%) of U.S.-born Latinos also preferred to identify themselves by the land of their ancestors instead of as "American."[29] This data elicits the following question to which I will now turn: What factors reinforce Hispanic ethnic identity, especially among native-born English-dominant Latinos with higher levels of acculturation and assimilation?

Perpetual resident aliens. Recently a number of experts have attempted to define the identity of Latinos in the United States. In *The Hispanic Condition: The Power of a People* Ilan Stavans, a first-generation Mexican Jew, reminds us that as Latinos "ours is an elusive identity—abstract, unreachable, obscure, a multifaceted monster."[30] The epigraph at the beginning of this chapter contains a quote from Virgilio Elizondo that resonates with many Latinos because it recalls our unenviable status in the United States as *perpetual resident aliens*, people referred to as "foreigners in their native land."[31] Our identity is inextricably tied to our history with and in the United States. As Stavans has noted, "ours isn't just another immigrant's story."[32] Unlike other immigrant groups, Hispanics are not newcomers to this country. Our earliest ancestors never crossed the border into the United States; instead Anglo Americans crossed the borders into our lands, lands settled by

---

[29]Ibid., p. 24.

[30]Ilan Stavans, *The Hispanic Condition: The Power of a People* (New York: HarperCollins, 2001), p. 24.

[31]David J. Weber, *Foreigners in Their Native Land: Historical Roots of the Mexican Americans*, rev. ed. (Albuquerque: University of New Mexico Press, 2004).

[32]Stavans, *The Hispanic Condition*, p. 245.

our Spanish forefathers long before the first English colonies were established in what later became the United States of America. Justo
González states it succinctly. "Actually, the first Hispanics to become
part of this country did not do so by migration but were rather engulfed
by the United States in its process of expansion—sometimes by pur-
chase, sometimes by military conquest, and sometimes by simple an-
nexation of territories that no one was strong enough to defend."[33] More
importantly, once "engulfed by the United States" a process of acculturation and assimilation began that some believe may never be fully
completed. This is partly due to the fact that we have always searched
for a way to undergo the processes of acculturation and assimilation
without losing *what* and *who* we are.

Polycentric identities. Juan Francisco Martínez reminds us that we
are people with different levels of identification with Latino culture
and with different levels of acculturation and assimilation to the
dominant group. This helps to explain the diversity and complexity of
Latino communities in the United States.[34] Martínez argues that Latino identity is fundamentally "polycentric and fluid." This means
that to a large extent Latinos can "opt for the level of identification
they want to have" with Latino culture and with the majority culture.
Martínez identifies several subgroups within the Hispanic community. Each represents a different level of identification with Latino
culture and with the majority culture. *Nuclear* or *monocultural Latinos*
are usually foreign born, Spanish dominant and live almost entirely
within a Latino community with very little contact with the majority
culture. *Bicultural Latinos* tend to be second-generation Latinos who
have chosen to maintain close ties to their roots within the Latino
community, but they can function equally well in the majority culture. *Marginal Latinos* have not completely distanced themselves from
Latino culture, but only occasionally identify with it. They may enjoy
Latino music and food but they live most of their lives in the world of

---

[33]Justo L. González, *Mañana: Christian Theology from a Hispanic Perspective* (Nashville: Abingdon, 1990), p. 31.
[34]Juan Francisco Martínez, *Walk with the People: Latino Ministry in the United States* (Nashville:
Abingdon, 2008), p. 18.

the majority culture. *Fleeing Latinos* include those attempting to escape from their ancestral culture. While they may not deny their Latino roots, they actively seek to become part of the dominant culture. *Returning Latinos* represent a fifth type, those who consciously desire to rediscover and strengthen their Latino identity. *Assimilated Latinos* include those who may identify themselves as Latino when it is convenient but culturally they live as highly assimilated members of the dominant group. A final option mentioned by Martínez identifies those Latinos who choose to become a part of *another culture* other than the majority culture—including Latinos who through marriage or because of racial identification are attracted to African American culture.[35]

Living in the hyphen. Most of us stand at the margin in some relationships and at the center in others.[36] As seen in each of the subgroups described above, this includes our relationships with Latino culture and with the majority culture in the United States. However, in most cases Latinos stand in a place somewhere between the centers of Hispanic culture and the majority culture. In his search for Latino identity in the United States, Ed Morales, a second-generation *Nuyorican*,[37] refers to this space "on the hyphen" as *Spanglish*.[38] The literal speaking of Spanglish is a survival mechanism, a way of importing the tongue of the adopted country while retaining the mindset of the old one.[39] But for Morales Spanglish is much more that what we speak; it is a metaphor for what we are doing, for how we act and how we perceive the world. In other words, Spanglish is another way to identify where we live: in the hyphen. "Spanglish is the ultimate space

---

[35]Ibid., pp. 21-22. See also Juan Francisco Martínez, "Acculturation and the Latino Protestant Church in the United States," in *Los Evangélicos: Portraits of Latino Protestantism in the United States*, eds. Juan F. Martínez and Lindy Scott (Eugene, Ore.: Wipf and Stock, 2009), pp. 109-113.

[36]Justo L. Gonzalez, *Santa Biblia: The Bible Through Hispanic Eyes* (Nashville: Abingdon, 1996), p. 33.

[37]*Nuyorican* refers to people of Puerto Rican ancestry born and raised in or near New York.

[38]Ed Morales, *Living in Spanglish: The Search for Latino Identity in America* (New York: St. Martin's Press, 2002), p. 97. Morales prefers the phrase "*on* the hyphen" rather than "*in* the hyphen," but makes no distinction between them. I will use the latter in the same manner as Morales uses the former.

[39]Ibid.

where the in-betweenness of being neither Latin American nor North American is negotiated. When we speak in Spanglish we are expressing not ambivalence, but a new region of discourse that has the possibility of redefining ourselves and the mainstream, as well as negating the conventional wisdom of assimilation and American-ness."[40] It is also important to recognize that new generations of Latinos born in the United States are generating hybrid cultures that combine the different realities they are experiencing, thereby creating a Hispanic context that is even more complex and diverse than what has been experienced in the past.[41]

Racial ambiguity. Professor Martínez is correct when he insists that a part of our identity as U.S. Latinos includes living in the hyphen "between the multiple influences that affect our identity."[42] Another important factor that influences and reinforces Hispanic ethnic identity is the racial ambiguity felt by many U.S.-born Latinos. Since 2000, the U.S. Census Bureau has asked informants to identify themselves by one or more racial categories, including White, Black or African American, Asian, American Indian and Alaska Native, and Native Hawaiian and Other Pacific Islander. However, since the U.S. Census Bureau has correctly observed that "People of Hispanic origin may be of any race," "Hispanic" or "Latino" is not offered as a separate racial category.[43] The trouble is that most "Latinos clearly indicate that they do not see themselves fitting into the five racial categories used by the U.S. Census Bureau and widely used elsewhere."[44]

Orlando Crespo, a second-generation Puerto Rican, sheds light on the racial ambiguity felt by many native-born Latinos including him and his siblings. "As a family we did not seem to fit into either Black or White categories of race. We simply saw ourselves as non-White, based on our Puerto Rican ethnicity."[45] While there are un-

---

[40]Ibid., p. 95.
[41]Martínez, *Walk with the People*, p. 28.
[42]Ibid.
[43]Betsy Guzmán, "The Hispanic Population 2000 Census Brief," C2KBR/01-3 (Washington, D.C.: U.S. Census Bureau, May 2001).
[44]Pew Hispanic Center and Kaiser Family Foundation, "2002 National Survey of Latinos," p. 31.
[45]Orlando Crespo, *Being Latino in Christ: Finding Wholeness in Your Ethnic Identity* (Downers

doubtedly white Latinos and black Latinos, many come from racially mixed backgrounds, including white, black and Native American or other indigenous strains.[46] Even within one family, by American standards one sibling may look black, another white, and another in between.[47] Thus for many Latinos, choosing a racial category "essentially amounts to having to deny a part of a Latino heritage or ancestral line that may have relatives that are near and dear."[48] According to Ed Morales, embracing Spanglish culture means not having to choose affiliation with a particular race. In other words, living in the hyphen is a space where multiple levels of racial and ethnic identification are possible.[49]

> Spanglish culture springs from a reaction to racism: in the case of the Caribbean Latinos, like Puerto Ricans and Dominicans, there is the refusal to let go of an African identity; in the case of the Mexican or Central American, there is a profound anchoring to the roots of the indigenous soul. It is an attempt to allow for multiple identification with the cultures of multiple races.[50]

Our multicultural, multiracial reality is not only confusing for us; our heterogeneity also perplexes the U.S. Census Bureau, which has been surveying Latinos to find a way to pinpoint us racially. Predictably, in 2000 when they were given the option to do so for the first time, 42 percent of all Latinos selected "Some Other Race." In 2002, when given the option to offer their own answer to the question of racial identity, almost half (47%) of all adult Latinos indicated that their *race* was "Hispanic" or "Latino."[51]

Grove, Ill.: InterVarsity Press, 2003), pp. 100-101.

[46]In 2010, 53 percent of the Hispanic population identified as white and no other race, 37 percent identified as some other race alone, and 6 percent reported multiple races. See Humes, Jones and Ramirez, "Overview of Race and Hispanic Origin: 2010," p. 6.

[47]Ibid.

[48]Melvin Delgado, *Social Work with Latinos: A Cultural Assets Paradigm* (Oxford: Oxford University Press, 2007), p. 18.

[49]Morales, *Living in Spanglish*, p. 17.

[50]Ibid., p. 50.

[51]Pew Hispanic Center and Kaiser Family Foundation, "2002 National Survey of Latinos," p. 32.

A CURIOUS THING ABOUT ETHNIC IDENTITY

The previous sampling of the research focusing on Hispanic ethnic identity suggests that acculturation and ethnic identity are distinct processes. By *ethnic identity* social scientists refer to a set of ideas one has about his or her own ethnic group membership.[52] More specifically, ethnic identity refers to knowledge of and personal ownership or membership in the group. It correlates knowledge, understandings, values and feelings that are direct implications of that ownership. Ethnic identity is thus an important domain of the self-concept, especially among minority and marginal groups.[53]

Surprisingly, Keefe and Padilla found that while cultural awareness declines from one generation to the next, ethnic identity becomes stronger, especially for those Mexican-Americans who live in large cities. That is, while "knowledge about" their culture declines and acculturation levels rise, their "feelings about" their ethnic identity intensify.[54] This would explain why many Mexican-Americans have persisted in celebrating traditional Mexican holidays such as *Cinco de Mayo* and *16 de Septiembre* (Mexican Independence Day) in spite of a growing lack of understanding of their original significance. These findings should caution us against assuming that the loss of cultural awareness about certain aspects of traditional culture (e.g., the true meaning of *Cinco de Mayo*) is accompanied by a loss of ethnic identity.[55] It would be more accurate to assume that among Latinos observing traditional Mexican holidays, "these days are a celebration of ethnicity."[56]

---

[52]Closely associated with ethnic identity is *ethnic identification*, which is defined as a psychological process in which people see qualities and characteristics in themselves that are similar to those they perceive in their group. *Ethnic consciousness* is typically treated as a broader concept that includes both ethnic identification and identity. See John A. Garcia, "Ethnicity and Chicanos: Measurement of Ethnic Identification, Identity, and Consciousness," *Hispanic Journal of Behavioral Sciences* 4 (1982): 298.

[53]George P. Knight and M. E. Bernal, M. K. Cota, C. A. Garza and K. A. Ocampo, "Family Socialization and Mexican American Identity and Behavior," in *Ethnic Identity: Formation and Transmission among Hispanics and Other Minorities*, ed. Martha E. Bernal and George P. Knight (New York: State University of New York Press, 1993), p. 106.

[54]Susan E. Keefe and Amado M. Padilla, *Chicano Ethnicity* (Notre Dame, Ind.: University of Notre Dame, 1987), p. 8.

[55]Norma Williams, *The Mexican American Family: Tradition and Change* (Dix Hill, N.Y.: General Hill, 1990), p. 81.

[56]Irene I. Blea, *Toward a Chicano Social Science* (New York: Praeger, 1988), p. 59.

THE EFFECTS OF DISCRIMINATORY TREATMENT

Social science research has confirmed that continued immigration from Latin America, the strength of familial ties, and discriminatory treatment in the United States reinforce Hispanic ethnic identity. The latter factor, discriminatory treatment, was found to generate intensive intra-group reliance and interaction and inhibit social contact with non-Latino-descent populations, and thereby has the inadvertent effect of reinforcing Hispanic ethnic identity.[57] In other words, when Latinos experience (or perceive) discriminatory treatment at the hands of the dominant group (i.e., non-Hispanic Whites or non-Hispanic Blacks) it strengthens ethnic loyalty and ethnic identity even among highly acculturated native-born Latinos. These findings become critical when one compares them with those of the 2002 National Survey of Latinos.

The 2002 study by the Pew Hispanic Center and Kaiser Family Foundation questioned nearly three thousand adult Latinos from various backgrounds and groups about experiences with and views about discrimination. Their findings reveal that "a large majority of Latinos feel that discrimination is a problem in general and that it is also a problem in specific settings such as schools and the work place."[58] Latinos reported that they experienced discrimination which prevented them from succeeding in schools and in the workplace, including not being hired for a job or not being promoted because of their race or ethnicity. Subtler forms of discrimination because of race and ethnicity included "being insulted or called names, being treated with less respect than others, and receiving poorer service than others." When asked to explain the reason for the discriminatory treatment, informants attributed it to their preference for Spanish, a pronounced accent in English and physical appearance.[59] Interestingly, native-born Latinos were more likely to attribute discriminatory treatment to their physical appearance.[60]

---

[57]Carlos H. Arce, "A Reconsideration of Chicano Culture and Identity," *Daedulus* 110 (1981): 171-91.

[58]Pew Hispanic Center and Kaiser Family Foundation, "2002 National Survey of Latinos," p. 70.

[59]Ibid., p. 69.

[60]Ibid., p. 80.

The Pew Hispanic Center and Kaiser Family Foundation study also found that the overwhelming majority of Latinos surveyed believe that discrimination by Latinos against other Latinos is also a major problem. They attributed this type of discrimination to socioeconomic differences, differences in country of origin and differences in skin color.[61] Likewise, in his brief but insightful book *Being Latino in Christ*, Orlando Crespo observes that foreign-born Latinos often discriminate against native-born Latinos based on what he calls "false measures used to define Latino identity." False measures used to determine who is truly a Latino include the following: physical features (i.e., Do you look Latino?), cultural habits (i.e., Do you listen to Latin music and prefer ethnic food?), geographic parameters (i.e., Do you live in the barrio?), religious parameters (i.e., Are you *católico?*), and of course language use (i.e., *¿Hablas español?*). If you answer negatively to any of these questions, especially the last one, your Hispanic ethnic identity is suspect, especially by some foreign-born Spanish-dominant Latinos.[62] In all fairness to foreign-born Latinos, native-born Latinos are also guilty of discriminating against Latino immigrants. When they do, reasons for discriminatory treatment cited usually include nativity, physical appearance and the inability to speak English well or at all.[63]

Drawing upon his own experiences as a U.S.-born Puerto Rican, Orlando Crespo observes that for native-born Latinos ethnic identity may be "tied less to language than to culture and values instilled in us that intermingle with our new culture in the United States." Nevertheless, many first-generation Latinos continue to look down on native-born Latinos because of their inability to speak Spanish well or at all.[64]

Insights gained from Daniel de Leon, senior pastor at *Templo Calvario* in Santa Ana, California, one of the largest multilingual multigenerational Hispanic churches in the country, coincide with those of

---

[61]Ibid., p. 72.

[62]Crespo, *Being Latino in Christ*, pp. 28-29.

[63]Pew Hispanic Center and Kaiser Family Foundation, "2002 National Survey of Latinos," pp. 80-82.

[64]Crespo, *Being Latino in Christ*, pp. 34-36.

Orlando Crespo. De Leon observes that the cultural and socio-economic barriers between immigrants and native-born Latinos are widened further when U.S.-born Latinos experience rejection at the hands of immigrants who criticize them for not speaking Spanish or for speaking it poorly.[65] Consequently, native-born Latinos do not usually respond favorably to the evangelistic efforts of Spanish-speaking immigrant churches where Latino ethnicity is most often determined by language use alone.

Nevertheless, when U.S.-born Latinos experience rejection at the hands of foreign-born Spanish-dominant Latinos, they seldom look for a surrogate church among non-Hispanic whites or non-Hispanic blacks. Native-born Latinos' status as perpetual resident aliens with polycentric identities, combined with the experience of living in the hyphen and of discriminatory treatment at the hands of the dominant group, creates a cultural as well as socioeconomic barrier between them and most churches of the dominant group. Informants consistently said that while they didn't always feel comfortable or welcomed in Spanish-dominant churches, they were equally reluctant to attend a predominantly white church. Instead, they preferred churches *con el sabor latino* (with a Latin flavor). This concurs with findings from a major study by the Pew Hispanic Center which found that among church-going Latinos, two-thirds attended what is referred to as an "ethnic church." An ethnic church is one that has three characteristics: at least some of the ministers are Latino, services are also available in Spanish and most of the members are Latino. Another fifth (21%) said that they respond positively to churches with two of the three characteristics. "These results show that a substantial majority of Latinos attend churches characterized by a distinctive Hispanic orientation."[66]

Clearly a moment of transition is upon us. The time has come for Hispanic denominational and church leaders to recognize that while Spanish continues to be acknowledged as "the language of intimacy

---

[65]Daniel de Leon, interview with author, March 22, 2007.
[66]Pew Hispanic Center, "Changing Faiths: Latinos and the Transformation of American Religion," Washington, D.C.: Pew Hispanic Center (April 2007), pp. 49-51.

and family," it is often not the language through which native-born
Latinos express their deepest thoughts and ideas, including their desire
to surrender to Jesus Christ as Lord and Savior.[67]

WHY FOCUS ON HISPANIC EVANGELICAL CHURCHES?

In this book I have chosen to focus attention exclusively on Hispanic
evangelical churches. The first main reason for this is personal. As a
nondenominational Christian associated with mainstream Churches
of Christ (non-instrumental), the definition of evangelical mentioned
in the introduction fairly accurately describes me.[68] The second reason
for focusing exclusively on Hispanic evangelical churches is demographic. Hispanic evangelicals greatly outnumber Hispanic mainline
Protestants and other types of non-Catholic Hispanic Christians.
Survey research has found that among all Latinos broadly described as
"Protestant," almost three in four identify themselves as evangelical or
"born-again."

According to a 2007 study by the Pew Hispanic Center, 92 percent
of all Latinos "profess a religious faith." As expected, more than two-
thirds (68%) of all Latinos report being Roman Catholic. Roughly one
in six (15%) identify themselves as evangelical or "born-again." Approximately one in twenty (5%) identify themselves as mainline Protestant (i.e., they do not say they are born again or evangelical). About one
in thirty (3%) identify themselves as belonging to "other Christian denominations." That is, they identify themselves as Jehovah's Witnesses,
Mormons or Orthodox Christians. Less than one percent (1%) said
they belonged to a non-Christian faith (e.g., Jewish, Muslim or another
non-Christian faith). Nearly one in ten (8%) identify themselves as
secular; that is, they say they have no specific religious affiliation or say
they are agnostic or atheist (see table 8).[69]

---

[67]Crespo, *Being Latino in Christ*, p. 35.

[68]Edward P. Myers, "Churches of Christ (A Capella), Are we Evangelical?" in *Evangelicalism and the Stone-Campbell Movement*, ed. William R. Baker (Downers Grove, Ill.: InterVarsity Press, 2002), p. 52.

[69]Pew Hispanic Center, "Changing Faiths," pp. 10-13; and Pew Hispanic Center/Pew Forum on Religion and Public Life, "PEW 2006 U.S. Religion Survey" (Washington, D.C.: Pew Hispanic Center, 2006).

Table 8. Religious Traditions Among Hispanics and Non-Hispanics

Among	Roman Catholic	Evangelical Protestant	Mainline Protestant	Other Christian	Secular	Don't Know/ Refused
All Hispanics	68%	15%	5%	3%	8%	1%
Native-born	58	18	8	3	10	1
Foreign-born	74	13	3	2	6	1
Non-Hispanics	20	35	24	3	11	2

Source: Pew Hispanic Center "Changing Faiths," 2007.

Findings from the 2007 study by the Pew Hispanic Center also suggest that native-born Latinos are more likely than foreign-born Latinos to describe themselves as evangelical Protestants.[70] Given my interest in outreach to native-born Latinos, focusing on Hispanic evangelical churches seems the logical choice, especially for a non-Catholic.

FROM *POCHO* TO PREACHER

Before we turn our attention to the case studies described in the next four chapters, let me describe an important episode in my own spiritual pilgrimage that may help readers better understand the rationale for this study.

For many years, our neighbors Jay and Alice Farris had tried unsuccessfully to share the gospel with my mother. But in the fall of 1971 our family suddenly found itself with nowhere to live and very few financial resources. To our surprise Jay and Alice and their four young daughters graciously opened their home to us. Our ongoing financial needs as well as the extraordinary generosity and genuine hospitality demonstrated toward us over the next two months made it more difficult to reject the invitations to visit their church. So, reluctantly, my mom fi-

---

[70]Pew Hispanic Center, "Changing Faiths," pp. 10-13. These figures are consistent with findings reported in a study by Catholic scholars who analyzed eleven national surveys conducted since 1990. Their findings suggest that approximately 70 percent of all adult Latinos are Catholic and that 20 percent are Protestant or other Christian. See Paul Perl, Jennifer Z. Greely and Mark M. Gray, "How Many Hispanics are Catholic? A Review of Survey Data and Methodology" (Washington, D.C.: Center for Applied Research in the Apostolate, Georgetown University, 2004).

nally agreed to go to church with them, at least once. Grudgingly, my three younger brothers and I joined her on that fateful visit in the fall of 1971. After all, we were Mexicans and Catholics! Why would we want to attend a white Protestant church? Fortunately we didn't know it at the time, but my mom, a twice-divorced single mother on welfare, and her four sons were among the first Latinos to ever step inside the College Church of Christ in Fresno, California.

Even though we felt like the proverbial "fish out of water," we were quickly astonished when several key members of this white middle-class nondenominational church immediately and wholeheartedly embraced us, responding in very practical and generous ways to the many physical, economic and spiritual needs our family had at the time. Perhaps more importantly, the immediate response of a few caring and influential members helped me to ignore what I perceived as some of the less enthusiastic responses to my family's presence.

The socioeconomic and cultural differences between my family and most of the members of the College Church of Christ fueled emotions and tensions that made me uncomfortable at times. For example, virtually no other teens in the youth group had to work, and those who did work were able to keep and spend all they earned. Like other working-class Chicanos, I worked to help the family make ends meet. I was also the only teenager wearing hand-me-downs from older members of the church's youth group. While other teens were driving Pontiac Firebirds and listening to Elton John, I was driving my *abuelo's* 1959 Chevy Impala while listening to Carlos Santana! But I didn't know of any predominantly Hispanic evangelical churches where a non-Spanish-speaking *pocho* would feel welcomed, so I stayed at the College Church of Christ where I was loved deeply by some very special people and where I grew to know and love the Lord Jesus Christ. I also came to know and love a young woman there named Jeanette Martin, who has been my loving and devoted companion since 1977.

In 1971, it would have been extremely difficult to find a predominantly Hispanic evangelical church in the United States that was successfully reaching English-dominant Chicanos like me. So I have often wondered how differently things might have turned out for me and my family had Jay and Alice been second-generation Latinos like my mom, and had their church been *la iglesia de Cristo en Fresno* instead of the College Church of Christ. As a kid growing up in Los Angeles and later as a Chicano teenager coming of age in central California, I learned from experience to avoid casual and personal encounters *con los recién llegados* (with recent immigrants). I feared they would engage me in a conversation and quickly discover that I didn't speak Spanish, that I was a *pocho*. I dreaded the inevitable disapproving glances and disparaging remarks like, "*¡Qué vergüenza!*" ("What a shame!"). Comments like those would trigger painfully familiar feelings of shame for not being able to speak Spanish, for being an *agringado*.

Fortunately, that was not my experience that first Sunday morning at the College Church of Christ in Fresno in 1971. Sadly, however, it continues to be the experience of countless numbers of U.S.-born English-dominant Latinos who walk into traditional Hispanic churches across the United States—where for the past 150 years of ministry among Latinos, most church leaders have assumed a Spanish-speaking immigrant-church model. This model still dominates the landscape of Hispanic ministries among Protestants, evangelicals, Pentecostals and nondenominational Christians in the United States. Unfortunately, this model is generally not successful when targeting the rapidly growing number of English-dominant Latinos.

Without a doubt, the initial visit to that white middle-class nondenominational church proved to be a turning point in the history of our broken and dysfunctional family. Today, two of my mother's sons (including myself) are ministers. My younger brother Michael is actually one of the pastors at the College Church of Christ in Fresno, a congregation that is now racially and ethnically diverse and boasts a large number of native-born English-dominant Latinos. My two sons and their wives are missionaries in China, and my mom's remaining sons and grandchildren are not only blessed beyond all we could have asked or imagined in 1971; more importantly, they are blessings to others in Jesus' name!

Nevertheless, my experience illustrates the challenges confronting many native-born Latinos faced with the choice of attending either a Spanish-only or Spanish-dominant (e.g., bilingual) church or a church of the dominant group. As the case studies that follow will demonstrate, most English-dominant Latinos usually prefer something in the middle, a church in the hyphen *con el sabor latino*. Thankfully, these case studies indicate that a increasing number of Hispanic church leaders do, in fact, recognize the significant differences that exist between foreign-born and native-born Latinos. They are also making courageous, creative and strategic adjustments to their church's programs and ministries to attract and accommodate the growing and diverse population of Latinos in the United States. They not only embrace the Great Commission (Mt 28:18-20) and the Great Commandments (Mk 12:29-31), they also affirm Hispanic ethnic identity and preserve *el sabor latino* in multilingual, multigenerational and multiethnic churches.

〰 2 〰

MULTIGENERATIONAL
HISPANIC CHURCHES

To the weak I became weak, so that I might win the weak. I have
become all things to all people, that I might by all means save some.
I do it all for the sake of the gospel, so that I may share in its blessings.

1 CORINTHIANS 9:22-23

THE GOSPEL OF JOHN RECORDS A PRAYER OF JESUS in which he inter-
cedes on behalf of his disciples at a critical moment of transition just
before his departure. After affirming his unique relationship with the
Father and the nature of his almost-completed mission on earth (Jn
17:1-5), the Lord begins interceding on behalf of his disciples as part of
the preparation for their historic mission in the world (Jn 17:6-19).
First, he prays for their protection in his absence (Jn 17:11-12, 15).
Then he prays for their unity (Jn 17:11). Next, Jesus prays that they may
experience his joy (Jn 17:13). Finally, he prays that the Father will ded-
icate them (i.e., sanctify them) for their mission (Jn 17:17-19). Then in
John 17:20 the Lord shifts his concern away from his twelve apostles
and focuses on others. He prays in the following manner, "I ask not
only on behalf of these, but also on behalf of those who will believe in
me through their word." On this passage Bruce Milne comments, "This
final section of Jesus' prayer is a deeply moving one because it brings
Jesus into direct relationship with us."[1] The point that must not escape
us is that as our Lord and Savior prays for the twelve apostles, he can

---

[1]Bruce Milne, *The Message of John* (Downers Grove, Ill.: InterVarsity Press, 1993), p. 247.

clearly envision generation after generation of disciples throughout the coming centuries and millennia, even down to our own age in the early twenty-first century. Jesus not only imagines future generations of disciples, but he can foresee their needs and he makes provisions for them through his prayer. "On our behalf" the Lord prays for supernatural unity (Jn 17:21-23), unity that will help persuade a rebellious world of the love of God revealed in Christ (Jn 17:23).

In praying in this manner, the Lord Jesus Christ reminds his disciples (and us as well) that despite all the challenges and trials that await them, their "mission is a profoundly hopeful activity."[2] His prayer also reminds the twelve, and servant leaders throughout the ages, that they too must pray for and provide for those immediately under their care. But Jesus' example in John 17 also reminds us that we must not neglect to pray for and make provision for future generations of disciples, including our children and grandchildren.

ON BEHALF OF THOSE WHO WILL BELIEVE IN JESUS

Earlier in this study we observed that when considering Hispanic ministry in the United States, many denominational and local church leaders continue to equate Hispanic ministry with ministry conducted almost exclusively in Spanish. While this model continues to be very effective for reaching and nurturing the faith of first-generation Latinos, it is generally not successful when targeting the growing number of native-born English-dominant Latinos in the United States. Instead, dedicated efforts by Spanish-speaking predominantly immigrant churches to evangelize and disciple unreached native-born Latinos are often hindered by linguistic as well as socioeconomic and cultural differences that exist between first-generation and U.S.-born Latinos.

Following the example of the Lord Jesus Christ in John 17, a growing number of dedicated and visionary first-generation Hispanic pastors have discovered creative ways to successfully minister to multiple generations of Latinos under the same roof. This chapter explores how linguistic, cultural and socioeconomic factors have reshaped ministry

---

[2]Ibid., p. 238.

paradigms and practices in several churches that traditionally targeted foreign-born Spanish-dominant Latinos but now *also* successfully target U.S.-born English-dominant Latinos. The remarkable success of these multilingual and multigenerational churches reveals that a commitment to serve, evangelize and disciple U.S.-born Latinos obliges church leaders to embrace more contextually appropriate ministry models for English-dominant Latinos who often feel out of place or even unwelcome in churches that are exclusively Spanish speaking, but who are also reluctant to assimilate into English-speaking dominant-group churches.

Personal interviews with pastors and lay leaders at each of the churches highlighted in this chapter reveal several common objections and obstacles that must be faced by those with similar visions, goals and objectives. As I will demonstrate in the case studies provided, one of the most common obstacles ultimately concerns defining the "mission" or purpose of the church. Is it the church's responsibility to help preserve the language, culture and traditions of the immigrant generation? Or is the task of the church best described by Paul in 1 Corinthians 9:22: to "become all things to all people, that [we] might by all means save some"? The answer to this question revolutionized the ministry paradigms in the churches described below.

Iglesia del Redentor/Church of the Redeemer, Baldwin Park, California

Established in 1961, *Iglesia del Redentor* was one of the first Spanish-speaking evangelical churches in southern California to transition to a multilingual, multigenerational model. The catalyst for change was founding pastor Aureliano Flores, a first-generation Mexican-American who as early as 1962 began to sense "the moment of transition." As his children began to grow and attend local public schools in Baldwin Park, Pastor Flores noticed a trend he had been observing in other Hispanic families: his children were becoming acculturated and assimilated into the dominant group, preferring to speak English instead of Spanish. Later, as preteens and teenagers, the Flores children often preferred to visit the English-speaking churches of their school friends rather than attend their father's church.

During this time Pastor Flores wrestled with the difficult options he faced. He could maintain the status quo and inevitably see his children leave for an English-speaking church. Worse still, he could watch them leave the church entirely, a common occurrence among children and grandchildren of other families in his congregation. On the other hand, he could make the necessary and difficult changes to adapt his ministry to the linguistic and cultural needs and preferences of his children and other U.S.-born Latinos. Torn between keeping his family together and maintaining the status quo, Pastor Flores sought the guidance of the Lord. According to Pastor Flores, the Lord reminded him, "I didn't call you to preach the gospel in English or Spanish. I called you to preach the gospel." So for the love of the gospel and for the love of his family he was compelled to change, resulting in a dynamic and thriving five-hundred-member multilingual church where three generations of the Flores family now serve the Lord together.[3] The church now offers separate worship services in Spanish and English on Sunday. At midweek gatherings Spanish and English services are held simultaneously at different locations on their three-acre urban campus.

When asked what made the initial decision so difficult, Flores responded, "I knew that I would have to become proficient in both languages, and since I didn't speak English very well, I would have to be humble, disciplined and work very hard." Pastor Flores's decade-long commitment to become proficient in English was driven by his belief that jealousy and distrust were certain to plague a multilingual church if it became necessary for him to delegate responsibility for the English group to an assistant. Instead, he chose to make himself vulnerable, learning to laugh at himself whenever he made mistakes while preaching and teaching in English.

Today Pastor Aureliano Flores is completely fluent in English and an inspiration to many other pastors, especially to his son Paul, who served as associate pastor for more than ten years. When his father announced that he would be retiring in 2008, Paul was asked to as-

---

[3]Aureliano Flores, interview with author, June 6, 2007.

sume the role of senior pastor. Anticipating his future role as senior pastor at Church of the Redeemer, Paul Flores has dedicated himself to becoming as proficient in Spanish as his father became in English. Like his father, Pastor Paul Flores is convinced that in order to maintain unity in a two-language church there must be one vision, and it is the pastor's duty to cast and nurture that vision, which he cannot do unless he is fluent in both English and Spanish.[4] Like his father, Pastor Paul Flores now leads a multigenerational Hispanic church where language is no barrier.

*Ministerios Coral Park/*Coral Park Ministries, Miami, Florida

Also known as *Primera Iglesia Bautista de Coral Park*, *Ministerios Coral Park/*Coral Park Ministries was launched in 1977 and is led today by Cuban-born Senior Pastor Luis Aranguren. In 2007, Aranguren was invited to return to *Ministerios Coral Park* by Senior Pastor Jorge Comesañas, a visionary who saw the need to transition the historic Spanish-only congregation into a multigenerational, multilingual church that would successfully reach out to the English-speaking community as well as to English-dominant Latinos. Pastor Comesañas recognized that the critical transition to the next stage in the history of the predominantly Cuban congregation would require the patient but courageous and intentional leadership of a fully bilingual and bicultural pastor—one who had the respect of the church, especially of the older immigrant generation, but who could also relate well to the younger generation of English-dominant Latinos. Luis Aranguren, who had faithfully served the church as an associate pastor in the 1990s before taking a position with a major Southern Baptist publishing house, was just such a person.[5]

Since returning to *Ministerios Coral Park*, Pastor Aranguren has encouraged and promoted the development of ministries and programs in English. He has also continued to challenge the belief held by many members that "it is the duty and responsibility of the church to teach the Spanish language to their kids." Instead he insists that it is the sa-

---

[4]Paul Flores, interview with author, June 6, 2007.
[5]Luis Aranguren, interview with author, June 28, 2008.

cred duty of the church to glorify God and preach the gospel to everyone, using whatever means necessary. In the case of younger U.S.-born
Latinos like his own children, this includes using English rather than
Spanish.[6] "Due to the diversity in our community, Coral Park Ministries offers everyone, of every age, the opportunity to worship God,
study the Word and serve others by means of the English language."[7]

Today Coral Park Ministries serves almost two thousand people in
their programs and services at the church's main campus in Westchester,
a neighborhood of Miami. In response to continued immigration from
Latin America and the Caribbean, Pastor Aranguren believes that for
the foreseeable future there will also be a continued and urgent need for
Spanish-language ministries. In fact, the church's new campus in Ken-
dall offers services in Spanish only. However, demographic trends in
south Florida suggest that the need for churches to respond to the linguistic preferences of the growing population of English-dominant Latinos will only increase in the coming years. Consequently, Coral Park
Ministries offers services in both English and Spanish on their main
campus. Average attendance at the Spanish service is about fifteen
hundred, while the English service averages nearly two hundred. Attendance at the English service has continued to grow since 2007, especially since the service was moved to a more conducive venue in a large
auditorium adjacent to the main sanctuary, where the Spanish service
takes place simultaneously. The English ministries pastor has also been
given the freedom to adapt his services so that they are contextually
relevant for the highly assimilated English-dominant Latino audience.
The attire is more casual and the music contemporary. In a historic
move, the newest campus in Cutler Bay is currently only offering services in English. Here Coral Park Ministries has had success reaching
a large number of Jamaicans in addition to English-speaking Latinos.[8]

When other pastors approach him and express their desire to follow the
example of churches like Coral Park Ministries, Aranguren is quick to

---

[6]Ibid.

[7]*Ministerios Coral Park*, "English Ministries," accessed on June 27, 2008 <www.coralpark.org/
english.html>.

[8]Aranguren, interview.

remind them of their sacred duty to embrace and minister to the entire family, including those who are highly assimilated and prefer to speak English. "Because it will require a lot more work, pastors must count the cost." For example, it will require many church leaders to leave what Aranguren calls their "ministry comfort zones." More importantly, it will usually require pastors to break with many of the longstanding and cherished traditions of their congregations and denominations. When "ministry boundaries" (i.e., traditional ministry paradigms and church culture) are challenged, church leaders must anticipate resistance from members who oppose the changes. Aranguren has observed that when long-time members become angry with the proposed changes and threaten to withhold their tithes or even leave the church, many pastors acquiesce and maintain the status quo. However, he is convinced that in most cases "the boundaries that pastors put in their minds are the only things holding them back from making the necessary adjustments in their ministries."

To those pastors trying to cast a vision for a multigenerational, multilingual Hispanic church among resistant older members and recent immigrants, Pastor Aranguren makes the following recommendations. First, love your church. "Invest your heart and soul in their lives. Unless your church is absolutely certain that you love them and that you want what is best for them, you will have a very difficult time implementing the desired and necessary changes." Second, be patient but intentional. Aranguren speaks of "intentional gradualism." He urges Latino pastors to make gradual but strategic changes over an extended period of time. *Ministerios Coral Park* started by first offering Sunday school classes in English for older elementary students, then for the teens, and later for young adults. Shortly thereafter, English-speaking small groups were added to the church's existing life groups. Only later did a separate Sunday morning English service get established. In addition, Luis Aranguren encourages pastors he mentors to stay well connected to each language group. "Preaching several times a year in the English service gives me a chance to remind those in the English service that along with the Spanish-speaking group, we are one church."[9]

---

[9]Ibid.

Iglesia Alpha & Omega/**Alpha and Omega Church, Miami, Florida**
Miami is a city of more than three million people, half of whom are
Latinos, and the majority of those of Cuban ancestry. So it is not
surprising that Miami is home to over three hundred Hispanic
churches, almost all of them exclusively Spanish speaking. Among
the largest and most visible Hispanic churches in Miami is *Iglesia
Alpha & Omega*, led by founding pastor Alberto Delgado, a former
refugee from Cuba, who launched the church in 1984 with just
twenty people. Today, *Iglesia Alpha & Omega* is a church of approximately six thousand members, 80 percent of whom are of Cuban ancestry, and many are immigrants like their pastor. Considered one of
the most respected, dynamic and successful Latino pastors in the
United States, Alberto Delgado surprised many in his church when
in 2004 he reversed his longstanding conviction that Alpha and
Omega would continue to be a Spanish-only church and announced
that the church would expand and encourage the use of English,
especially among the youth and young adults. He also announced
plans to begin a Sunday morning worship service in English to meet
the needs of U.S.-born members of the church and their non-Latino
spouses and friends.

When asked what caused him to initiate the unprecedented changes
in his ministry, Pastor Delgado recalled attending a three-day conference for Hispanic pastors in Long Beach, California, hosted by the
Alianza de Ministerios Evangélicos Nacionales (AMEN), a multidenomi-
national association of Hispanic Protestant leaders in the United States.
Pastor Delgado was surprised and disturbed when the entire conference
was conducted in English, in spite of the fact that virtually every one of
the more than one thousand people present was Latino. Interacting with
dozens of participants at the conference, he learned that many of the
pastors served Hispanic churches where English was now the primary
and sometimes the only language used. Like many other pastors and
denominational leaders who are highly critical of Hispanic pastors who
use or encourage the use of English, Delgado initially concluded that
the conference reflected the context of Mexican-American churches in
southern California rather than a national trend that would anytime

soon impact Cuban-Americans and other Latinos in South Florida.[10]

Closer to home, another factor was to have an enormous impact on Pastor Delgado's decision to transform *Iglesia Alpha & Omega* into a multilingual and multigenerational Hispanic church. He had recently become a grandfather and observed sadly that in spite of his life-long insistence that his children speak to him in Spanish, his U.S.-born adult children only spoke to one another, their peers and his grandchildren in English. To those who questioned his judgment, Delgado responded frankly, "If we do not adjust [our approach] we run the risk of losing our children and grandchildren to the world."[11]

Mike Castillo, young adult pastor at *Iglesia Alpha & Omega*, agrees with his pastor. Castillo believes that historically, English-dominant Latino Christians have had two unappealing choices. They could choose to attend the Spanish-dominant churches of their parents and *abuelos* (grandparents), where they are often "forced to speak Spanish and hammered when they don't," and where they feel out of place and even unwelcome because they are considered too anglicized. As a result of the way they feel and are sometimes treated in traditional Hispanic churches many English-dominant Latinos choose to leave the churches of their parents and *abuelos*. Some of those who leave may choose to attend a dominant-group church. But for many highly assimilated Latinos this too is an unattractive choice because in predominantly Anglo churches they often feel "uncomfortably conspicuous, insecure and outnumbered."[12] Now, however, there are a growing number of Hispanic churches in south Florida like *Iglesia Alpha & Omega* that have added English language ministries and programs. In many cases, the decision to respond to the language preferences and unique cultural background of English-dominant Latinos has helped to halt the exodus of teens and young adults from the churches of their ancestors.

After three years, the Sunday morning English service at *Iglesia Alpha & Omega* draws a little more than three hundred people. But attendance is slowly climbing as members now recognize that they have

---

[10]Alberto Delgado, interview with author, June 27, 2008.
[11]Ibid.
[12]Mike Castillo, interview with author, June 30, 2008.

a place to invite their English-dominant children and grandchildren as well as their non-Latino friends and neighbors. Pastor Delgado, who preaches at this service and at two additional services in Spanish every Sunday, is confident that the attendance in the English service will rise dramatically in the coming years. The Friday night youth service now draws more than four hundred teens weekly to a service that freely uses "Spanglish" and incorporates rock and salsa music to communicate the gospel to English-dominant Latino youth, *con el sabor latino*.[13] To those who raise objections about the use of English and contemporary music in youth gatherings, Delgado responds insightfully, "the message is more important than the language or the genre of music used to communicate it."[14]

Reflecting on his earlier observations at the AMEN conference he attended in California, Pastor Delgado now insists, *"vamos a llegar a pasar lo mismo aquí"* ("We are going to experience the same thing [in Miami]"). His vision is to build a church where multiple generations of Latinos (English and Spanish speaking) as well as non-Latinos *se sientan en casa* (will feel at home).[15]

*Vida Abundante/*Abundant Life Church, San Antonio, Texas

San Antonio, Texas, is home to one of the largest, oldest and proudest Hispanic populations in the United States. It was the first major U.S. city to elect a Hispanic mayor and is home to a number of thriving and pioneering Hispanic evangelical churches. Several, including *Vida Abundante*, have a vision for reaching multiple generations of predominantly Mexican-descent Latinos on the Southside of San Antonio. Since coming to *Vida Abundante* in 1998, Pastor Elieser Bonilla, a first-generation Mexican married to a first-generation Dominican, has seen his multisite Church of God (Cleveland, Tennessee) congregation grow from 350 to approximately 2,000 members in the past ten years. The

---

[13]Manuel Ortiz, *The Hispanic Challenge: Opportunities Confronting the Church* (Downers Grove, Ill.: InterVarsity Press, 1993), p. 62. Ortiz defines *Spanglish* as a new functional language that incorporates both Spanish and English by juxtaposing Spanish grammatical structure on English-based words, thereby permitting U.S.-born Latinos to develop an identity unique from those of their parents or the dominant group.

[14]Delgado, interview.

[15]Ibid.

church's phenomenal growth followed the decision to suspend a four-year experiment with various models of bilingual services in favor of separate services in English and Spanish. The historic decision was based primarily on the needs and preferences of the English-dominant members who were generally less tolerant of the bilingual services and generally unwilling to use headsets. Today the Spanish service is averaging one thousand in attendance, while the English service is averaging six hundred. Interestingly, the new north campus which opened in 2008 averages four hundred for their bilingual service. Pastor Bonilla insists that as soon as the north campus is strategically prepared to do so they will suspend the bilingual service and begin offering two separate services, as they currently do on the main campus.[16]

Even though the majority of those in his multisite congregation are immigrants or children of immigrants, Pastor Bonilla recognizes that native-born English-dominant Latinos represent the largest portion of the Hispanic population in San Antonio. From experience he is also aware that language is only one barrier between the foreign-born and native-born members of his church and community. There are also significant socioeconomic and cultural differences that cause many native-born English-dominant Latinos to look elsewhere when they discover that the north campus is bilingual. Similarly, many of those who currently form the core of the membership at the north campus say they remain there because of loyalty to the church and its vision and because they know that in the not-too-distant future separate English and Spanish services are coming. Bonilla recognizes that because of its proximity to the border, there will always be a need for Spanish-speaking congregations in San Antonio. Nevertheless, he is convinced that if he chose to embrace a Spanish-only model, he would be limiting his congregation's ability to reach and attract the majority of San Antonio's Latino population, which is native born and English dominant.[17]

It should also be noted that critical to the successful transition from bilingual to separate English and Spanish services was the transition to a cell-based model. The small group ministry at *Vida Abundante* thrives

---

[16]Eliezer Bonilla, interview with author, June 18, 2009.
[17]Eliezer Bonilla, interview with author, December 11, 2009.

in part because as the church grew larger, it was simultaneously growing smaller, with the majority of its members participating in one of more than three hundred language-specific and gender-specific homogeneous small groups. Pastor Bonilla believes that "a thriving cell group ministry" mitigates the stress during the transition from a bilingual to a multilingual format because "fundamentally people are not looking for meaningful worship as much as they are looking for meaningful relationships. When meaningful relationships in the church are being nurtured in the context of intimate small groups, little else matters."[18]

New Life Covenant Church, Chicago, Illinois

Pastor Wilfredo De Jesús, a second-generation Puerto Rican, was born and raised in the Humboldt Park neighborhood of Chicago, where he grew up a Roman Catholic in a working-class family with an alcoholic father. In 1977, at the age of fifteen, Wilfredo landed a summer job with the City of Chicago. To his surprise Wilfredo was assigned to assist *Templo Cristiano Palestina*, a small Hispanic Pentecostal church offering a Vacation Bible School (VBS) for inner-city kids. During the VBS he was impressed by the commitment and passion of the church's youth. Not long after that summer, Wilfredo gave his life to the Lord and began attending *Templo Cristiano Palestina*, where he soon became a lay youth leader.

In 1988 Wilfredo married his high school sweetheart, Elizabeth Marrero, the pastor's daughter. A year later, because of his commitment, charisma and leadership skills, Wilfredo was invited to become the church's youth minister. In 1998 Senior Pastor Ignacio Marrero announced his plans to retire in 2000. Wilfredo was asked by Pastor Marrero, the board of elders and the congregation of approximately 125 members to assume the role of senior pastor upon his father-in-law's retirement. However, before Wilfredo would agree to serve as the church's new pastor he proposed a fundamental shift in the congregation's traditional approach to ministry. He insisted that if the church was to reach and serve the entire community, it must immediately begin incorporating English in all its programs and services to meet the linguistic preferences of Latinos who

---

[18]Ibid.

love *la comida criolla* (Puerto Rican food) but prefer to speak English. Initial fears, resistance and reluctance to agree with the proposed changes were mitigated by the trust and confidence that Pastor Wilfredo De Jesús earned during twenty years of faithful and loyal service to the church and to his mentor, Pastor Marrero.

The fears of older, Spanish-dominant members were addressed patiently, respectfully and directly. According to Pastor Wilfredo, their biggest fear was that they would be pushed aside and inevitably be left behind by the younger, English-dominant majority. Wilfredo assured them that as their new pastor he would continue to serve every member of the church, but that he had been called by God to serve the entire community of Humboldt Park, including people from diverse linguistic and cultural backgrounds. Interestingly, all the board meetings where this historic change was being discussed were conducted in English, reflecting the dominance of the native-born members of the church.[19] Not long after the change, the church was renamed "New Life Covenant Church," reflecting the goal and source of the church's new vision, "To be a Christ-like congregation that transforms the community into a NEW LIFE."[20]

In 2009 New Life Covenant Church averaged over five thousand in attendance for its five services offered in the auditorium at Roberto Clemente High School in the heart of Humboldt Park. Four of the five weekend services are offered in English. However, even in the English-language services one can easily perceive the *Boricua*[21] influence in the music, prayers and preaching. The one Spanish service averages over five hundred in attendance, far more that the 125 members who were attending the Spanish-only services of *Templo Cristiano Palestina* in 2000. Pastor De Jesús preaches weekly at all five services, staying true to his commitment not to neglect the Spanish-speaking members of the church. Nevertheless, the demographic makeup of the church is slowly changing, reflecting the diverse community in Humboldt Park.

---

[19]Wilfredo De Jesús, interview with author, May 23, 2008.
[20]New Life Covenant Church, "Mission and Vision," accessed on May 16, 2008 <www.mynewlife.org/Content.aspx?content_id=9545&site_id=10087>.
[21]Puerto Ricans commonly refer to themselves as *Boricua*.

Today, 80 percent of the membership at New Life Covenant Church is still Latino, the overwhelming majority of whom are native-born and English-dominant. But non-Latino friends and spouses of members are also finding Christ at New Life Covenant Church.

THE REJECTED GENERATION

Lay leaders and young Hispanic pastors like Dave Serrano in the South Bronx look at the example of churches described in this chapter with hope that other Hispanic churches, including his own, will soon respond in similar ways to the needs of younger U.S.-born Latinos like him. However, he still imagines that most U.S.-born Latinos will find traditional Hispanic churches dominated by immigrants from Puerto Rico, Cuba or Mexico who outwardly appear more concerned with preserving their language and culture heritage than with the spiritual well-being of younger native-born Latinos.[22]

Equally disappointing is the fact that dominant-group churches have also failed to attract the growing number of U.S.-born Latinos. Though they usually prefer to speak English and have an affinity for things American, many second- and later-generation Latinos nonetheless perceive that they are treated as second-class citizens in the country of their birth and often treated as outsiders in the churches of the dominant group. Furthermore, many church leaders do not understand that even though the linguistic and cultural distance between U.S.-born Latinos and the dominant group has been minimized due to a preference for English and higher levels of acculturation, the legacy of 150 years of cultural conflict, marginalization and discrimination has alienated many U.S.-born Latinos from institutions of the dominant group, including the church.

Justo González, a leading Latino Protestant theologian, has noted that in spite of the fact that 60 percent of all Latinos are American citizens by birth, many native-born Latinos are none the less "made to feel as if they are newcomers."[23] This makes the burden of change in

---

[22]Dave Serrano, interview with author, May 21, 2008.
[23]Justo L. González, *Santa Biblia: Reading the Bible Through Hispanic Eyes* (Nashville: Abingdon, 1996), p. 93.

the traditional Hispanic church all the more essential, because as González has observed, "the church is part of the gospel itself. The gospel, the good news, is not only that our sins are forgiven and we are reconciled with God; it is also that we are *citizens* and *family* with the saints and with God! It is in the church that we experience that."[24]

As denominational and local church leaders prayerfully consider the examples presented here as well as the needs of present and future generations of native-born Latinos, the apostle Paul's example is instructive. In 1 Corinthians 9:19-23, the apostle Paul defends himself against accusations that he lacks integrity—acting one way and teaching one version of the gospel when in the company of Jews, but acting another way and preaching what appeared to be a different gospel when among Gentiles. To this mistaken understanding of his character, intentions and message, Paul informs his critics that he is actually motivated by a desire to win more people to Christ, whether Jews or Greeks. He insists, "I do it all for the sake of the gospel" (1 Cor 9:23). Similarly, the motives and actions of the pastors and churches described in this chapter have been questioned and second guessed by friends and critics alike. So what motivated the pastors and churches highlighted in this chapter to break with the status quo?

FACTORS THAT INFLUENCED THE TRANSITION

The pastors and churches highlighted in this chapter were influenced by multiple factors to begin separate programs and services in English. Most were motivated by a desire to keep Hispanic families (including their own) together under one roof. They were also motivated by a commitment to provide for the spiritual well-being and development of the English-dominant youth and young adults. Each pastor was also motivated by a desire to grow, which each church did almost immediately, some remarkably.

Dr. Isaac Canales, senior pastor at Mission Ebenezer Family Church in Carson, California, identified additional factors not mentioned by the pastors in this chapter, including a desire to broaden the economic

---

[24]Ibid., p. 109.

base of the congregation. According to Pastor Canales, "you cannot build a great or financially independent church on the back of immigrants." He insists that Hispanic leaders, who desire to be free of denominational control or the control of a sponsoring church, must reach out strategically to upwardly mobile native-born Latinos.[25]

OBJECTIONS THAT MUST BE OVERCOME

To implement the changes described above, these visionary pastors and church leaders had to respond to numerous critics, including those whose understanding of the nature and mission of the local church stood in contrast to the leaders'. Below I've listed a few of the most common objections raised when pastors began to address the needs and preferences of native-born English-dominant Latinos in contextually relevant ways.

We must preserve our language and culture! To those who were trying to pressure and manipulate the apostle Paul to conform to their cultural and theological preferences, Paul responds, "I am free with respect to all," yet for the cause of Christ "I have made myself a slave to all, so that I might win more of them" (1 Cor 9:19). In *Hispanic Realities Impacting America*, Daniel Sánchez has observed that in a similar manner many immigrant parents pressure their pastors to help them "preserve the Hispanic language and culture."[26] In response to the pressure to assume tasks not given by God to the church, these case studies reveal bold, courageous leadership that is not afraid to upset a few "to win more of them." Frustrated and anxious immigrants often counter their determined pastors with, "We've never done it that way before!" In response to this objection, pastors try to help reluctant members to recognize that they are often more concerned with conserving their ancestral culture and language than with the spiritual welfare of their children and grandchildren.

It will separate our families! Unconvinced, many members object to separate English services by insisting that "it will separate our fami-

---

[25]Isaac Canales, interview with author, March 15, 2007.
[26]Daniel R. Sánchez, *Hispanic Realities Impacting America: Implications for Evangelism & Missions* (Fort Worth, Tex.: Church Starting Network, 2006), p. 85.

lies." This is precisely what happened in 2002 when Victor Rodríguez, senior pastor at South San Filadefia Church in San Antonio, Texas, announced plans to abandon the church's bilingual model and begin offering two services, one in Spanish and another in English. Pastor Rodríguez was convinced that the 150-member church was limiting its growth with bilingual services. Earlier in his ministry, bilingual services appeared to be an acceptable way to keep families together as well as to attract English-dominant Latinos and their non-Latino friends, spouses and extended family members. But before long Rodríguez observed that the logistics of bilingual services not only exhausted the pastoral staff and worship team, but they also left many members and guests frustrated and bored. Some complained that they were not being adequately fed (spiritually) in bilingual services. Others expressed impatience with the process. As a result, many members still expressed reluctance to invite unchurched family members and friends to the bilingual services at South San Filadefia Church. Rodríguez also realized that the resistance from native-born Latinos to bilingual services was not just linguistic. Spanish-only and bilingual services still reflected efforts to respond to the culture and needs of the immigrant generation rather than the context of native-born Latinos. Since making the historic change in 2002, the nine-hundred-member South San Filadefia Church has become one of the fastest-growing churches in the Baptist General Convention of Texas. Rodríguez is not surprised that many of the church's new members are the children and grandchildren of the older immigrant generation.[27]

The devil speaks English! Still others object that promoting the use of English will open the door for Satan to enter via "the decadent culture of the Anglos." Pastor Isaac Canales recalls hearing members object, *"el diablo habla ingles"* ("the devil speaks English"), revealing the sense of "cultural superiority" endemic among many traditional and conservative first-generation Latinos. One of the most common objections heard by Canales was that promoting English would undermine the social and moral integrity of the congregation, especially among

---

[27]Victor Rodríguez, interview with author, July 27, 2008.

the youth who would inevitably begin thinking and acting like Anglo teens. Canales reminded skeptical members that drug and alcohol abuse, disrespect for parents, juvenile delinquency and sexual promiscuity were just as common among teens in Spanish-only churches; in other words, *"¡el diablo es bilingüe!"* ("the devil is bilingual!").[28]

Once they determined that the transition to a multilingual, multigenerational model was God's will for their ministries, pastors faced additional challenges. First, they had to face the reality that some of those who disagreed with their decision would leave the church. Second, Spanish-dominant pastors confessed that they were initially afraid of the hard work and humility required in learning to preach and teach equally well in English.

Still more challenging for many first-generation pastors was the need to recognize that the differences and barriers between English and Spanish-speaking Latinos is not just linguistic but also cultural—requiring them to make adjustments in the music and style of preaching they were accustomed to using with first-generation Latinos. During his teen and young adult years at Primitive Christian Church on the Lower East Side of Manhattan, Pastor Marc Rivera recalls watching many young Latinos leave the church, not so much because of the exclusive use of Spanish, but because they were turned off by the indefensible legalism and traditionalism that still characterizes many Hispanic Pentecostal churches.[29] Pastors and churches like those highlighted in this study revisited their historic stances on a multiplicity of subjects, including the prohibition against women wearing pants to church. Each ultimately made the bold and strategic decision "to no longer bind culturally informed traditions and prohibitions on its members and guests."[30]

BY ALL POSSIBLE MEANS

As he reflected on the arduous task of accommodating his ministry and message to different audiences, the apostle Paul reminded his readers

---

[28]Ibid.
[29]Marc Rivera, interview with author, May 20, 2008.
[30]Ibid.

that it was worth the effort. "I have become all things to all people, that I might by all means save some" (1 Cor 9:22). The profiles of the leaders described in this chapter reveal that it takes not just hard work, sensitivity and flexibility to become all things to all Latinos; it takes courage, patience and determination to meet the inevitable criticism from those who prefer that things stay as they are, even at the expense of their children and grandchildren's spiritual welfare. Here again the example of the apostle Paul is instructive. He reminds his critics that his modus operandi may not win him their approval, but it will help him to share in the blessings of bringing more people to Christ (1 Cor 9:23). Similarly, the pastors and churches highlighted in these case studies long ago gave up trying to impress their peers or denomination leaders. Their satisfaction appears to come from pleasing God, even if it means challenging their culture's norms of acceptability, for the sake of becoming all things to all Latinos.

∿ 3 ∿

MULTIETHNIC, PREDOMINATELY HISPANIC CHURCHES

Now when Jesus heard that John had been arrested,
he withdrew to Galilee. He left Nazareth and made his home in
Capernaum by the sea, in the territory of Zebulun and Naphtali, so that
what had been spoken through the prophet Isaiah might be fulfilled: "Land of
Zebulun, land of Naphtali, on the road by the sea, across the Jordan, Galilee
of the Gentiles—the people who sat in darkness have seen a great light, and
for those who sat in the region and shadow of death light has dawned."
From that time Jesus began to proclaim, "Repent, for the
kingdom of heaven has come near."

MATTHEW 4:12-17

IN HIS STUDY OF THE CHALLENGES facing the Hispanic church at the
dawn of the twenty-first century, Manuel Ortiz asked, "Will the
African-American, Asian or Anglo community be excluded from
hearing the gospel because we insist on speaking only Spanish in our
local churches?"[1] More recently, Juan Francisco Martínez has echoed
this challenge: "If a Latino church is going to take its missional responsibility seriously, it needs to find ways to minister among non-
Latinos." The challenge, then, is to find models in which predominantly Hispanic churches can be intentionally multiethnic and

---

[1]Manuel Ortiz, *The Hispanic Challenge: Opportunities Confronting the Church* (Downers Grove,
Ill.: InterVarsity Press, 1993), p. 109.

multicultural while still being sensitive to the complexity of the Latino experience in the United States.[2]

This chapter will highlight and analyze the efforts of several predominately Hispanic churches to rise to the challenge posed by Dr. Ortiz. Unlike the churches highlighted in the previous chapter, the churches described here all began initially targeting native-born English-dominant Latinos rather than foreign-born Spanish-speaking Latinos. This strategic decision would enable these churches to embrace non-Latinos, including African Americans, Asian Americans and Anglos, with various ties to the neighborhood and to Latino members of these churches.

One important difference between native-born and foreign-born Latinos is significant and worth mentioning again here: Foreign-born Latinos, like immigrants in general, tend to marry within their ethnic or racial group. However, this is not true of Latinos born in the United States. According to a recent study published by the Pew Hispanic Center, 32 percent of second-generation and 57 percent of third-plus generation Latinos marry outside of their ethnic or racial group.[3] Not only do many native-born Latinos marry non-Latinos, they also have a higher percentage of friends and extended family members who are non-Latino than do foreign-born Latinos. The churches highlighted in this chapter acknowledge this fact and adjust their models of ministry to accommodate a growing number of non-Latinos, including spouses, close friends, extended-family members and coworkers. Not surprisingly, these churches usually resist being categorized as "Hispanic churches." Instead, in an effort to reach a diverse audience that includes a growing number of non-Latinos, these churches prefer to describe themselves as "multiethnic, predominately Hispanic churches."

The case studies that follow fall into two categories. Churches in the first group specifically target at-risk communities and marginalized groups such as gang members, drug dealers, drug addicts, prostitutes

---

[2]Juan Francisco Martínez, *Walk with the People: Latino Ministry in the United States* (Nashville: Abingdon, 2008), p. 80.

[3]Robert Suro and Jeffrey S. Passel, "The Rise of the Second Generation: Changing Patterns in Hispanic Population Growth" (Washington, D.C.: Pew Hispanic Center, October 2003), p. 9.

and ex-convicts irrespective of their racial or ethnic background. The second set of churches successfully targets upwardly mobile, middle-class English-dominant Latinos. Each church understands its God-given task "is neither to destroy nor to maintain ethnic identities but to replace them with a new identity in Christ that is more foundational than earthly identities."[4]

MULTIETHNIC HISPANIC CHURCHES IN AT-RISK COMMUNITIES

In Luke 1 the elderly priest Zechariah, filled with the Holy Spirit, echoes a messianic text from Isaiah 9:1-2 when he speaks prophetically of the future ministry of his son John, forerunner to the Messiah. "By the tender mercy of our God, the dawn from on high will break upon us, *to give light to those who sit in darkness and in the shadow of death*, to guide our feet into the way of peace" (Lk 1:78-79, emphasis added). Three decades later, as Matthew explains the choice of Galilee for the inauguration of the Messiah's public ministry, he too recalls the same text from Isaiah, which he inserts in Matthew 4:15-16: "Land of Zebulun, land of Naphtali, on the road by the sea, across the Jordan, Galilee of the Gentiles—*the people who sat in darkness have seen a great light, and for those who sat in the region and shadow of death light has dawned*" (emphasis added).

"Those who sit in darkness and in the shadow of death" also describes the socioeconomic context of many Latinos in the United States today, especially the children of immigrants. Scholars at the Research and Resource Center for Hispanic Youth and Young Adult Ministry define children and teens most at risk as "those whose lives are surrounded by gangs and role models engaging in high-risk activities, and who need extra support at home and school to avoid falling into the traps of gangs, drugs, violence, and other criminal behavior."[5]

Victory Outreach International, Praise Chapel Christian Fellowship and New Harvest Christian Fellowship are three church-planting

---

[4]Paul Heibert, quoted in Manuel Ortiz, *One New People: Models for Developing a Multiethnic Church* (Downers Grove, Ill.: InterVarsity Press, 1996), p. 132.
[5]Ken Johnson-Mondragón, ed., *Pathways for Hope and Faith Among Hispanic Teens: Pastoral Reflections and Strategies Inspired by the National Study of Youth and Religion* (Stockton, Calif.: Instituto Fe y Vida, 2007), p. 37.

movements born in the barrio that strategically and successfully target those at risk in underserved inner-city neighborhoods across the United States. After providing a brief history and profile of each movement, I will take a closer look at their creative and holistic approaches to youth ministry and preaching. In a subsequent chapter I will return to discuss each movement's approach to indigenous leadership development in the context of the local church.

Victory Outreach International

Sonny Arguinzoni, the founder of Victory Outreach International (VOI), is a second-generation Puerto Rican born and raised in Brooklyn, New York. At the age of twelve Sonny decided he would never again go to his parents' "dull" and "legalistic" church.[6] Instead, Sonny became a heroin addict, gang member and ex-convict. But at the age of twenty-one, Sonny was miraculously cured of his six-year addiction to heroin and converted to Christ when he came into contact with ex–gang member Nicky Cruz and Teen Challenge, the ministry of David Wilkerson, author of *The Cross and the Switchblade*. In 1962 Sonny left New York to attend the Latin American Bible Institute (LABI) of the Assemblies of God in La Puente, California. While at LABI, Sonny began working with Teen Challenge in Los Angeles. After recognizing that most ex–drug addicts and former gang members did not "fit in" or were not welcomed in the typical Hispanic evangelical churches of the day, Sonny felt called by God to start a church for people rejected by many evangelicals as well as by society at large. In fact, those at Victory Outreach believe that God has promised to give them "the treasures [out] of darkness" (Is 45:3).[7]

In 1967 Arguinzoni and his small band of rejected disciples purchased a small church in Boyle Heights, a drug and gang-infested section of East Los Angeles, and began what was then called "Victory Temple Addicts Church." Since 1967 Victory Outreach has grown from a single inner-city church to a worldwide network of over six hundred

---

[6]Sonny and Julie Arguinzoni, *Treasures Out of Darkness* (San Dimas, Calif.: Vision Multimedia, 2000), p. 21.
[7]Sonny Arguinzoni, *Sonny* (San Dimas, Calif.: Vision Multimedia, 1987), pp. 92-137.

churches and ministries, with locations across the United States and in twenty-four countries from the Philippines to the Netherlands. The mother church in La Puente, California, now led by Sonny Arguinzoni Jr., has over four thousand members.[8] In addition to leading VOI for the past forty years, Pastor Sonny Arguinzoni has written an autobiography,[9] an anecdotal history of the movement,[10] and articulated its philosophy and vision of ministry.[11]

Today VOI is a comprehensive outreach and discipleship ministry that spans the globe, serving holistically in the name of Jesus. This is clearly evident in the movement's mission statement.

> Victory Outreach is an international church-oriented Christian ministry called to the task of evangelizing and discipling the hurting people of the world with the message of hope and plan of Jesus Christ.
>
> This call involves a commitment to plant and develop churches, rehabilitation homes and training centers in strategic cities of the world.
>
> Victory Outreach inspires and instills within people the desire to fulfill their potential in life with a sense of dignity, belonging and destiny.
>
> Victory Outreach works cooperatively with others of mutual purpose in accomplishing the task before us.[12]

Victory Outreach is unique in that it specifically targets the inner city, drug addicts, alcoholics, gang members, prostitutes, ex-convicts and other social outcasts.[13] As one might expect, Victory Outreach is a multiethnic and interracial movement. However, one of the first things an outside observer would notice is that the overwhelming majority of

---

[8]While most VOI churches tend to be between 100 and 300 members, others are quite large. For instance, Victory Outreach churches in San Bernardino and San Jose, California, have more than 1000 members.

[9]*Sonny* (1987) was originally printed under the titles *God's Junkie* and *Once a Junkie*.

[10]*Treasures Out of Darkness* (2000) was coauthored with Julie Arguinzoni. The first edition appeared in 1991. Nicky Cruz, longtime friend of Pastor Sonny, has written a sympathetic anecdotal history of VOI titled *Give Me Back My Dignity* (La Puente, Calif.: Cruz Press, 1993).

[11]Sonny Arguinzoni, *Internalizing the Vision* (San Dimas, Calif.: Vision Multimedia, 1995) was written to help members "catch the vision" of VOI.

[12]Victory Outreach International, "Values," accessed on May 30, 2007 <www.victoryoutreach .org/info/Values.asp>.

[13]Gastón Espinosa, "Victory Outreach International," in *The New International Dictionary of Pentecostal and Charismatic Movements*, ed. Stanley M. Burgess and Eduard M. Van Der Maas (Grand Rapids: Zondervan, 2002), pp. 331-32.

its members are second- and third-generation Latinos. While Victory Outreach resists referring to itself as a Hispanic, Latino or Chicano church, the demographics, including the overwhelming number of Hispanic pastors throughout the movement, cannot be easily overlooked. For example, seven of the denomination's eight elders, including Pastor Sonny, are Latinos, as are 75 percent of the thirty-nine regional pastors. If the demographic makeup of those currently enrolled in the movement's Urban Training Centers is any indication, leadership at Victory Outreach will continue to be dominated by native-born Latinos for years to come.

Praise Chapel Christian Fellowship

Unlike Sonny Arguinzoni, Mike Neville, founder of Praise Chapel Christian Fellowship (PCCF), was the son of a traveling evangelist. At the age of twenty-one Mike, with his brother Larry, followed in their father's footsteps and began to travel around the country conducting revivals of their own. Two years later the evangelistic team broke up when Mike married Donna McCamish, who was also raised in a preacher's home. For the next five years Mike and Donna were on the road as traveling evangelists. Then in May of 1976, the Nevilles packed up their family and belongings and moved from Tulsa, Oklahoma, to Maywood, a central city southeast of downtown Los Angeles, where Mike had been invited to become the pastor of a small Pentecostal church.

In his book *The Harvest Generation: The Story of Praise Chapel*, Praise Chapel historian Ron Simpkins states that the Nevilles' first year in southern California was filled with critical and strategic challenges and decisions. The effective evangelistic techniques, discipleship programs and church planting that would soon characterize the movement today known as Praise Chapel Christian Fellowship were still waiting to be discovered.[14] The most obvious challenge the Nevilles faced was demographic. The church building was located in a poor working-class Hispanic neighborhood, filled with drug dealers and terrorized by many

---

[14]Ron Simpkins, *The Harvest Generation: The Story of Praise Chapel* (Huntington Park, Calif.: Mission Global Harvest Press, 1994), p. 14.

dangerous inner-city gangs. Soon after his arrival church members were urging the new pastor to move the church to a safer suburb further east of downtown. But after receiving a revelation from God to the contrary, Pastor Mike stood before the congregation and made the following announcement: "Churches should reflect the communities they are in, and ours doesn't. We are going to have drug addicts and prostitutes, as well as lawyers [in this church]. . . . This church is going to be filled with Hispanics." Immediately twenty members walked out; many others would follow during the course of the Nevilles first turbulent year in Maywood.[15]

But according to the home church's official website, "many young gang members gave their lives to Christ and a sovereign wave of revival swept through the community." Pastor Mike immediately began to disciple the young and predominately Latino converts and soon began to see the congregation stretching out beyond the four walls of the church. In 1980 the first "pioneer church" was planted forty miles east of Maywood in Ontario, California. Since that time, over two hundred churches have been planted across the United States and hundreds more in thirteen nations.[16]

In 1996, after leading Praise Chapel for more than twenty years, Mike Neville died after a brief but courageous battle with brain cancer. His wife Donna assumed the role of senior pastor of the mother church that had since moved to nearby Huntington Park. Mike Neville's brother Larry became the president of Praise Chapel Christian Fellowship International, now headquartered in Rancho Cucamonga, California.

The official policy manual describes Praise Chapel as "a church multiplication movement" whose stated vision is "Win, Build, and Send." Their purpose is articulated in the following three statements: "Preach and teach the gospel of Jesus worldwide," "Plant churches domestically and internationally," and "Fellowship together with other churches, ministries and fellowships with like minded vision." Their vision is articulated in the following statement: "To reproduce and mul-

[15]Quoted in ibid., p. 16.
[16]Praise Chapel Huntington Park, "About Us," accessed on October 18, 2009 <www
.praisechapelhp.com/aboutus.html>.

tiply churches and fellowships of churches, providing ongoing discipleship training and spiritual leadership for continued development and fruitfulness."[17]

Like Victory Outreach, Praise Chapel resists referring to itself as a Hispanic ministry or Hispanic denomination, but fellowship leaders including President Larry Neville and cofounder and Senior Pastor Donna Neville agree that well over 80 percent of the movement's North American members are Latino, while more than 90 percent of its pastors are Latino.[18] This includes many of its pastors serving overseas.[19] For the foreseeable future in the United States, Praise Chapel will continue to be dominated by native-born Latinos.

New Harvest Christian Fellowship

Originally known as Victory Chapel, New Harvest Christian Fellowship (NHCF) began humbly but passionately in 1974 when twelve adults began meeting in a small two-bedroom home in La Puente, California, a predominately Hispanic suburb east of downtown Los Angeles. From the beginning, the inspirational contemporary music that continues to characterize New Harvest attracted many people to the church who might not otherwise have had a chance to be exposed to the word of God. A steadfast commitment to Spirit-led and life-transforming prayer also continues to define this Pentecostal movement almost forty years later. Knowledgeable outsiders who seldom or never attend a service at New Harvest would probably say that besides its reputation for stirring and contemporary Christian music, the movement is known for its ongoing dedication to serving the communities in which the churches are located.[20]

In 1980 the name of the movement was changed to New Harvest Christian Fellowship and the "mother church" moved to its present

[17]Praise Chapel Christian Fellowship, *Policy Manuel 2006* (Rancho Cucamonga, Calif.: PCCF, 2006), p. 3.

[18]Donna Neville, interviews with author, March 22, 2007, and November 7, 2007; Larry Neville, interview with author, April 5, 2007.

[19]See a list of PCCF pastors at <www.praisechapel.com/international/pccfonline.php>.

[20]New Harvest Christian Fellowship, "The Story of New Harvest," accessed on December 12, 2009 <www.newharvestnorwalk.com/index.php?option=com_content&view=article&id=109&Itemid=159>.

location in Norwalk, a central-city suburb of southeast Los Angeles known for its drug-related crime and gang activity. Currently, the mother church has a membership of more than one thousand and guides a fellowship of more than fifty "satellite churches" across the United States and in several foreign countries including England, Honduras, Mexico and Russia. The church in Norwalk is led by Senior Pastor Richard Salazar, a second-generation Mexican-American who was one of the original members of the movement in 1974.[21] Under the leadership of Pastor Salazar, the mother church continues to set the standard for the movement, not only in its inspired and relevant worship services, but perhaps more importantly in its dedication to serving the community beyond the walls of the church.

Like Victory Outreach, New Harvest runs many men's and women's rehabilitation homes that give "yesterday's hopeless an opportunity to become tomorrow's productive world citizens." Rehabilitation homes provide free food and shelter, biblical counseling, a twelve-step recovery and a high school graduation program. A strict discipline of supervised work, anger management and coping skills allows for progressive recovery.[22]

Under Pastor Salazar's leadership, New Harvest started Family Outreach and Community Intervention Services (F.O.C.I.S.), a 501(c)(3) that allows the church to collaborate with various local and national programs designed to focus attention on the urgent and habitual problems that plague the community, including poor health and health care, gang-related violence, and physical and emotional abuse as well as substance abuse. "F.O.C.I.S. offers a comprehensive network of programs and activities that complement one another, resulting in a consistent source of hope and security for the community it serves."[23]

Reflecting the demographics of the communities they serve, most New Harvest churches in the United States remain overwhelmingly Latino. Since the highest priority at New Harvest is reaching at-risk

---

[21]Ibid.

[22]New Harvest Christian Fellowship, "About Us," accessed on December 12, 2009 <www .newharvestoneighty.com/about_us.htm>.

[23]F.O.C.I.S., "Services," accessed on December 12, 2009 <http://focisweb.com/>.

youth, the majority of those served at New Harvest are native-born English-dominant Latinos who continue to invite and bring their non-Latino friends to the programs and ministries of the church. This in turn attracts more non-Latino parents who are at first curious but later grateful for the assistance provided them by the church. Pastor Salazar acknowledges that "in the early days" the main focus was on Latinos, but now New Harvest attracts a growing number of non-Latinos and therefore resists referring to itself as a Hispanic church-planting movement, preferring the term "multiethnic church."[24]

In a matter of three to four decades, Victory Outreach, Praise Chapel and New Harvest have successfully planted hundreds of healthy and evangelistic churches across America in at-risk Hispanic neighborhoods, targeting second- and third-generation Latinos. Recently, however, each movement has also begun to successfully plant churches that target Latin American immigrants, as many of their target neighborhoods have experienced an influx of first-generation Latinos during the past two decades. But through experience each movement has learned to appreciate the cultural as well as linguistic differences that separate the immigrant generation from native-born Latino generations. Thus Spanish and English fellowships within each movement usually work independently of one another. Nevertheless, in spite of the cultural and linguistic barriers, Spanish and English congregations in each movement share a common vision and purpose. Yet the overwhelming majority of programs and ministries offered at VOI, PCCF and NHCF continue to be conducted in English, making it easier for each to attract young native-born English-dominant Latinos.

YOUTH MINISTRY IN THE SHADOW OF DEATH

It was noted earlier in this study that the Hispanic population is much younger than the rest of the U.S. population. For example, the average age of non-Hispanic whites in 2007 was 40, while the average age for Latinos was 27. The average age drops significantly when considering only native-born Latinos, who made up 61 percent of the Hispanic population.[25]

---

[24]Richard Salazar, interview with author, December 14, 2009.
[25]Richard Fry and Jeffrey S. Passel, "Latino Children: A Majority Are U.S.-Born Offspring of

Massive immigration that began in the 1980s continues to impact the Hispanic communities. Latinos now make up 22 percent of all children under the age of 18 in the United States. In 2009 a study by the Pew Hispanic Center noted that the size of the second generation has quadrupled between 1980 and 2007. Of the 16 million Latinos under 18 years of age, 52 percent (8.2 million) are second generation, 37 percent (6 million) are third generation or higher while only 11 percent (1.7 million) are foreign born. This means that almost 90 percent (14.2 million) of all Latinos under the age of 18 are U.S. citizens by birth. It comes as no surprise that 82 percent of all Latinos between 5 and 17 years old speak English very well. In fact, 32 percent speak only English in the home (see table 9).[26]

Table 9. Characteristics of Children, by Race, Ethnicity and Generation Status

Characteristic	All	All Latinos	First Gen.	Second Gen.	Third+ Gen.
Total (in millions)	73.9	15.3	1.5	7.6	5.3
Gender					
Male	51	51	53	51	51
Female	49	49	47	49	49
Age Groups					
Younger than 5	28	32	8	35	34
5-14	54	53	62	53	53
15-17	18	15	30	12	14
Language (ages 5-17 only)					
Speaks only English in the home	80	32	4	12	68
Speaks English very well	15	50	54	67	27
Speaks English less than very well	5	18	43	21	5
Poverty Status					
Not Living in poverty	82	73	66	74	76
Living in Poverty	18	27	34	26	24

Source: Pew Hispanic Center "Latino Children" (May 2009)

Immigrants" (Washington, D.C.: Pew Hispanic Center, May 2008), p. i.
[26]Ibid., p. 3.

This data suggests that ministry among Latinos must give special attention to youth, especially to those living at or below the poverty line in at-risk urban neighborhoods where most Latinos live. This is precisely what one observes at Victory Outreach International, Praise Chapel Christian Fellowship and New Harvest Christian Fellowship congregations in barrios across the country.

Youth ministry at Victory Outreach. Since 1967 Victory Outreach has been creating a "legacy of hope" for thousands trapped in drug addiction, prostitution and the gang lifestyle. But Victory Outreach is much more than drug rehabilitation programs or gang prevention programs. In youth programs throughout the movement, they are now training a new generation of committed young people who have never been drug users yet have a burden to serve the inner cities. "God's Anointed Now Generation" or G.A.N.G. is a revolutionary, faith-based approach to getting teens and young adults away from the mindless destruction of street gangs, the "tattooed warriors who are spreading the culture of alienated urban Latino youth."[27] Low-rider car shows, Christian rap and hip-hop concerts, and live stage productions are used as vehicles for communicating the gospel in contextually relevant ways. More than a simple youth ministry, G.A.N.G. challenges teens to do great things for God and for Victory Outreach.[28] A popular jingle heard around Victory Outreach captures the spirit and vision of this ministry: "We are not the X, we're not the Next, we're not the New, we are the Now Generation!"

In 1994 Victory Outreach launched the first of several "Urban Training Centers" (UTCs) to provide extensive one- and two-year training programs for young adults wanting to go into full-time ministry. Many of those involved in G.A.N.G. and the UTCs are the children of ex-addicts converted through Victory Outreach. Many of these young men and women have gone on to start group recovery homes, drug treatment centers, urban intervention programs, churches, prison visitation outreaches and family counseling centers. The "second generation," as

---

[27]See the official VOI website at <www.victoryoutreach.org/ministries/victory-outreach-youth .asp>.

[28]VOI publishes *G.A.N.G. Life Magazine.*

they are often referred to, is infusing Victory Outreach with new energy and modern methods to reach teens and young adults in the world's inner cities.

Youth ministry at Praise Chapel. Since its early days in Maywood, Praise Chapel has demonstrated a consistent commitment to "win, train and send" teens and young adults into the "global harvest" in their own backyards as well as overseas. Praise Chapel youth ministries are known by such provocative names as "Armed and Dangerous," "Go 4 It Youth," and "Souled Out Youth Ministries"—clearly sensitive to their inner-city target group. Adam Friedrich, youth pastor at Praise Chapel in the City of Orange, exemplifies the creative and daring youth ministries typical of the movement. Besides offering an after-school program to help teens stay out of trouble and stay in school, Adam's staff operates a skateboard park and a weekly Christian hip-hop competition that attracts hundreds of teens and young adults. He also organizes domestic and foreign mission trips to places where teens assist pioneer church planters with cutting-edge evangelistic dramas depicting life in the barrio without Christ, and hip-hop concerts targeting unchurched inner-city teens.[29]

Youth ministry at New Harvest. Recognizing that "the youth we reach today will be the leaders of tomorrow," New Harvest Christian Fellowship has implemented even more creative outreach ministries to attract at-risk teens in inner-city neighborhoods.[30] "Oneightywest" is the dynamic and creative ministry at New Harvest that challenges youth ages thirteen to twenty-two to "do a one-eighty." Saturday nights from six to nine p.m., teens from the area surrounding Norwalk gather in a state-of-the art venue equipped with a video game arcade and a skate park. All services, including food, transportation, a live DJ, concerts and dramas are provided free of charge.[31] Through this exciting cutting-edge ministry teens are encouraged to enroll in an eight-week discipleship course that challenges them to embrace the rule of Jesus

---

[29]Adam Friedrich, interview with author, March 30, 2007.
[30]New Harvest Christian Fellowship, "About Us."
[31]Oneightywest, "Welcome to Oneightywest," accessed on December 12, 2009 <www.oneighty west.com/>.

Christ over every area of their lives. The course concludes with graduates taking a vow of abstinence until marriage, and to remain drug and alcohol free. For those teens already struggling with chemical dependency and other related problems, New Harvest offers a recovery program appropriately called "Life Hurts, God Heals." "The B.E.A.T." (Building Excellence and Achievement in Teens) is a mentoring and tutoring program at New Harvest designed to inspire academic excellence and build uncompromising character in teens who are struggling to succeed or stay in school. For those who are unable to succeed in the local public schools, "New Harvest School" (grades K-12) gives students deemed "hopeless cases" another chance to finish high school while increasing their self esteem and building character.[32]

Youth and young adult ministries at Victory Outreach, Praise Chapel and New Harvest represent contextually appropriate responses to a generation of at-risk Latinos in the United States, particularly among those living in underserved inner-city neighborhoods.

PREACHING THE GOSPEL IN THE SHADOW OF DEATH

Latino Catholics are also trying to understand the success of church-planting movements like Victory Outreach, Praise Chapel and New Harvest. Bishop Robert González of Boston examined the nature of the message preached by charismatic and Pentecostal groups like Victory Outreach, Praise Chapel and New Harvest in order to better understand their attraction to large numbers of Latinos. His research question was quite simple: What are they saying? González summarized what he understands as a message rooted in the gospel, a message that presents Christ in all his power as the foundation of new life, of conversion, of forgiveness of sins. In his words, "Their preaching seems to be based solely upon the person and power of Christ. They preach the sovereignty of Christ. They preach it enthusiastically, whereas we seem to be tired followers of Christ."[33]

---

[32]New Harvest Christian Fellowship, "What we Offer," accessed December 12, 2009 <http://www.newharvestoneighty.com/what_we_offer.htm>.

[33]Robert O. González, O.F.M., Auxiliary Bishop of Boston, MA, "The New Evangelization and Hispanics in the United States," *America*, October 19, 1991, p. 268.

At Victory Outreach, Praise Chapel and New Harvest the gospel is not just preached enthusiastically, it is preached boldly. In his book *Internalizing the Vision* (1995), the unofficial ministry manual for Victory Outreach, Pastor Sonny Arguinzoni yearns for more men and women with initiative and vision, who will preach the gospel with boldness and enthusiasm. "Spreading the gospel requires boldness. Because of our boldness, we're able to move into the worst neighborhoods of some of the world's roughest cities with aggressiveness, dedication and effectiveness."[34]

Rick Alanis, pastor of an eight-hundred-member Victory Outreach church in San Bernardino, California, has launched sixteen churches in sixteen years. His young pastors are "launched out" to preach boldly and enthusiastically that Jesus Christ has the power to deliver people from life-controlling habits and broken lives. According to Pastor Rick, boldness and enthusiasm flow from the integrity of the messenger. He asks, "How can you preach the message of deliverance if you yourself have not been delivered?"[35]

At Victory Outreach, Praise Chapel and New Harvest, Christ's liberating power and sovereignty is preached by men and women transformed by that power who now live abundant lives under his rule. The preaching one hears at Victory Outreach, Praise Chapel and New Harvest validates Bishop González's conclusion that evangelical churches that attract Latinos preach the gospel enthusiastically and boldly.[36] When bold, Christ-centered preaching is validated by creative worship and ministries that respond in contextually appropriate ways to the needs of people living in the shadow of death, the results are often nothing short of amazing.

UPWARDLY MOBILE MULTIETHNIC HISPANIC CHURCHES

Within traditional Hispanic neighborhoods and their surrounding communities one can also find a growing Hispanic middle class. As

---

[34]Arguinzoni, *Internalizing the Vision*, pp. 76-77.
[35]From a video-recorded message delivered during the VOI World Conference at the Long Beach Convention Center (August 26, 2000).
[36]González, "The New Evangelization," p. 268.

one might expect, a much larger percentage of upwardly mobile Latinos are native born and English dominant. Because of their higher educational attainment levels they are more likely to serve in professional or managerial positions, and therefore usually earn considerably more than foreign-born Spanish-dominant Latinos. As was noted earlier, social science research reveals that these socioeconomic factors have been correlated positively with higher levels of acculturation. This means that native-born Latinos are generally more assimilated to the dominant culture than foreign-born, poor and working class Latinos who tend to live at the margin of the dominant group and its institutions. Nevertheless, many upwardly mobile Latinos still gravitate to institutions that are predominately Hispanic, especially where English is the language of preference. Such institutions, including churches, often serve as a bridge to life and opportunities outside of the barrio. The case studies that follow reveal the evangelistic potential inherent in predominately Hispanic English-speaking churches strategically poised and ready to cross racial and ethnic barriers without losing their *sabor latino* (Latino flavor) among upwardly mobile native-born Latinos.

Calvary Fellowship, Miami Lakes, Florida. In 2000 founding pastor Bob Franquiz received what he believed to be a God-given vision "to establish a church that teaches the Bible in relevant and creative ways" in South Florida. Pastor Bob, a second-generation Cuban-American, recognized that a large and fast growing segment of Miami's young Latino population was native-born and English-dominant. But virtually all the Hispanic churches in the area were either bilingual, Spanish-dominant or Spanish only. Beginning with seven people gathered in a living room, Calvary Fellowship was launched as a church where everyone, regardless of their ethnic or racial background, would be welcome. Today Calvary Fellowship is a church of approximately six hundred members who celebrate their life together in Christ on Sunday mornings in the auditorium at Everglades High School in Miramar, Florida.

When asked why more than 90 percent of the church's members are Latino, Pastor Bob believes it is because they feel comfortable. He recalls a comment made by a new member who stated that "the people here understand my family and background, the unique tensions and situations we face as Latinos." This understanding was simply but profoundly demonstrated when the church put up a banner to advertize the times and place of their weekly gatherings. The banner read, "Calvary Fellowship: Not Your *Abuela's* Church!" The implication was loud and clear: this is a church where people love Jesus just as much as your *abuela* does. Yet it isn't targeting her, but someone with an *abuela* (i.e., a Latino), and someone who also speaks English. According to Pastor Bob, "The banner spoke a lot about who we are and what we are trying to do." At Calvary Fellowship room is made for everyone's cultural baggage, including the tensions and situations faced by native-born English-dominant Latinos surrounded by immigrants from Latin America who cherish their homeland, culture and language. But room is also made for members' preferences for things American, including rock music, a staple at Calvary Fellowship.[37]

Pastor Mark Rodríguez, a second-generation Cuban-American, is responsible for worship and the youth ministry at Calvary Fellowship. Before joining the church-planting team headed by Pastor Bob Franquiz, Pastor Mark was actively involved at two different evangelical Hispanic churches in South Florida. His experience mirrors that of many second-generation Latinos who make their way to Calvary Fellowship. On the one hand he has a *sentir* (special feeling) for things *cubano*. But on the other hand he more fully embraces the American Dream and American cultural values than many among the immigrant generation.

For many among the foreign born, the corrupting influence of the dominant group's values is only reinforced by the use of English. Consequently, prior to coming to Calvary Fellowship Pastor Mark Rodríguez remembers being discouraged from speaking English, especially at church. So today it doesn't surprise him when he looks out on his growing youth group and sees young Latinos who were formerly members at nearby churches where the use of English was discouraged. Pastor Mark regularly sees whole families, including parents who barely speak English, transfer to Calvary Fellowship because they

---

[37]Bob Franquiz, interview with author, July 3, 2008.

see their children more enthusiastically embracing the gospel and growing in the grace of God.[38]

According to Pastor Bob Franquiz, there are no plans to add programs or services in Spanish. Those who desire or need them have many excellent Spanish-only or bilingual churches to choose from in the community. According to Pastor Bob, Calvary Fellowship is committed to "doing the same thing we did when there were just seven of us. We are seeking to help people take their next steps towards God. No matter where you are in relationship to God: you could be a fully committed follower of Jesus or someone who doesn't have any kind of relationship with God. We all have a next step to take to get closer to God. We simply want to help you take yours."[39]

Over the past few years Calvary Fellowship has become ethnically more diverse, reflecting the demographics of the neighborhood. Nevertheless, words or phrases in Spanish naturally make their way into sermons and classes taught by Pastor Bob and his staff. Without alienating non-Latinos in the audience, these comments elicit laughter and what Pastor Bob calls a "sense of connection" that hopefully causes members and guests to muse, "These people understand where I'm coming from." After services at Calvary Fellowship, it is common to hear members and guests speaking in English making plans to meet at a local Cuban restaurant to enjoy *picadillo* (Cuban beef hash) and *moros y cristianos* (black beans and rice) before driving away in their cars listening to rock music. This certainly isn't your *abuela's* church.

Calvary Chapel, Montebello, California. Three time zones and twenty-seven hundred miles away, Pastor Pancho Juárez has been nurturing one of the largest English-speaking Hispanic churches in Southern California. The campus of Calvary Chapel Montebello is just a few miles from downtown Los Angeles and the tough urban neighborhoods where Pancho grew up after immigrating from Mexico when he was eleven years old. Like so many young Latino immigrants, spending

---

[38]Mark Rodríguez, interview with author, July 3, 2008.
[39]Calvary Fellowship, "About Us—History," accessed on December 30, 2009 <www.calvary wired.com/about_history.php>.

countless hours listening to R&B (rhythm and blues) on the radio and watching American television not only helped Pancho learn to speak English, it also caused him to become "culturally detached" from his family.[40] Assimilating quickly, it didn't take long for Pancho to find his way along what he calls "a crooked path" filled with drugs and illicit sex. His reckless lifestyle was only exacerbated by a stint in the Marine Corps during the Vietnam War.[41]

In 1975 Pancho's girlfriend Millie came in contact with the ministry of Chuck Smith, pastor of Calvary Chapel in Costa Mesa, a church at the center of the Jesus Movement of the 1970s. Refusing her initial efforts to share the gospel with him, Pancho accepted her invitation to attend a rock concert, which to his surprise turned out to be at Calvary Chapel! But that night he made the decision "to give God a chance."[42] Shortly thereafter, Pancho and Millie were married, started raising a family and began attending the Calvary Chapel in West Covina, where Pastor Raul Ries spent eleven years nurturing Pancho's faith. In 1989 Pancho enthusiastically agreed to lead a Friday night home Bible study in the predominately Hispanic community of Montebello. By 1991 the home fellowship had grown to two hundred people and Pancho was named the pastor of what in 1992 would officially become Calvary Chapel Montebello, a church "disposed to reach to the down-and-outs, the outcasts, and those who were basically tired of a deep-cultured, dead-religion."[43] Today Calvary Chapel in Montebello averages more than three thousand in attendance on Sunday mornings, where Pastor Pancho preaches to three services packed with English-dominant Latinos and a small but growing number of non-Latinos, including boyfriends, girlfriends, spouses, extended family, friends and coworkers of members.

From the moment you enter the gated parking lot or board a shuttle from one of the satellite parking lots, the atmosphere at Calvary Cha-

---

[40]Pancho Juárez, *An Altered Life* (Montebello, Calif.: Calvary Chapel of Montebello, 2005), pp. 20-21.

[41]Ibid., p. 2.

[42]Ibid., p. 69.

[43]Calvary Chapel Montebello, "An Altered Life," accessed on December 31, 2009 <www.ccmtb .com/index.php?P=11>.

pel Montebello is casual yet reverent. Before, between and after its three Sunday services, a bookstore and coffee shop help guests feel welcomed to "hang out" at church as they would at a shopping mall during the holidays. A corps of greeters and ushers are there to show newcomers around and introduce those with children to the converted warehouse that is home to a well-organized, child-friendly Sunday school program that welcomes and teaches more than a thousand children every Sunday.

Besides offering state-of-the-art programs for children and youth, one unique way that Pastor Pancho has found to impact the at-risk neighborhood surrounding his church is by offering his services and church building for funerals for known drug dealers and gang members killed on the streets of Los Angeles. Family members and close friends of these despised outcasts are often surprised by the dignity and respect Pastor Pancho and his staff show the deceased and those who grieve for them. Mourners are frequently given personal autographed copies of the pastor's autobiography (e.g., personal testimony), titled *An Altered Life*. Mourners are also sincerely encouraged by their sensitive hosts to attend one of the church's regular functions. Many do.[44]

Within blocks of the campus of Calvary Chapel Montebello several traditional Spanish-speaking evangelical churches can be found catering almost exclusively to immigrants looking for *paisanos* (compatriots) who share their culture, values and language in a strange and often hostile environment. Justo González maintains that for a growing number of these foreign-born Latinos, the "church becomes a new extended family, in a way that the dominant culture finds difficult to understand!"[45] But in southern California, where there has been a significant Hispanic presence for over two hundred years, a much larger number of Latinos are native-born and less comfortable in Spanish-speaking, predominately immigrant churches. Into the vacuum of churches targeting more highly assimilated, English-dominant Latinos, Pancho Juárez and Calvary Chapel Montebello have come target-

---

[44]Pancho Juárez, interview with author, January 28, 2007.
[45]Justo L. González, *Santa Biblia: Reading the Bible Through Hispanic Eyes* (Nashville: Abingdon, 1996), p. 109.

ing those looking for Jesus Christ in a church with a distinctive Latino flavor where everyone is welcome, regardless of their race or ethnicity.

Waves of Faith, Fort Worth, Texas. Rey Martínez is a fourth-generation Mexican-American who serves as the founding and lead pastor at Waves of Faith, a Southern Baptist church in Fort Worth, Texas. When asked why he chose to plant an English-dominant church in Fort Worth he said, "I knew there were other people like me, Hispanics who don't fit in at traditional Spanish-speaking congregations. Yet like me, when they go to predominately Anglo congregations, they don't feel like they really fit in there either."[46] Furthermore, he had a vision of reaching African Americans and whites as well as English-speaking unchurched Latinos. His goal was not to plant a Hispanic church, but to plant "a dynamic, multicultural local body that offers relevant teaching and amazing worship as part of each and every service," where committed disciples—not just church members—would be made of everyone, regardless of their ethnic background.[47]

In 2000 the new church plant began meeting in a renovated warehouse in an industrial park in south Fort Worth. The "come as you are" approach at Waves of Faith is characterized by a relaxed non-threatening and non-institutional atmosphere. For the sake of making guests feel at home at programs and services at Waves of Faith, Pastor Rey encourages members to dress casually, and to avoid traditional greetings like "good morning, Hermano Martínez," and anything else that might unnecessarily cause guests to feel uncomfortable or out-of-place. Critics have accused Rey Martínez and Waves of Faith of "watering down the gospel" for the sake of popularity and numerical growth. He insists that he is not watering down the gospel. "This is not about my preferences or your preferences, it is about getting back to the Great Commission" and about embracing the apostolic example of "becoming all things to all people" for the sake reaching the lost. "We must go where the people are and not where we want them to be." According to Pastor Rey, this means being willing and ready to "compromise our

---

[46]Rey Martínez, interview with author, July 22, 2008.
[47]Waves of Faith, "What to Expect," accessed December 3, 2009 <www.wavesoffaith.com/what.php>.

local church culture" just as one would do who was going overseas as a foreign missionary. "Here in south Fort Worth, we are in a mission field and the same missionary principles apply." Today Waves of Faith averages more than 250 in attendance on Sundays, including 140 "covenant members," 85 percent of whom are Latino, most of Mexican ancestry. Other members are equally divided between African Americans and whites.[48]

The attitude and vision of Pastor Rey Martínez sounds very similar to that of the late Orlando E. Costas, who insisted that "to make disciples means in the first place, to lead woman and men to follow Jesus. . . . This involves surrendering to his care one's life ambitions, personal needs and group loyalties."[49] At Waves of Faith loyalty to the Great Commission supersedes allegiance to traditional forms and patterns, making it possible for the church to respond in culturally relevant ways to its target audience.

FaithWorld International Church, Chicago, Illinois. In 1991 Daniel Cruz, a second-generation Puerto Rican, and twenty other English-speaking Latinos gathered in a borrowed sanctuary to launch what is known today as FaithWorld International Church in the Humboldt Park neighborhood on the Westside of Chicago. FaithWorld is a church committed to "Loving God, Growing Together, Giving of Ourselves, Serving our Community." Through successful programs like "Adopt-a-Block," FaithWorld lives out its motto and has continued to grow steadily. Today attendance in their four weekly services has exceeded 1,100; more than 80 percent are Latino. In 2002 FaithWorld successfully launched a daughter church in nearby East Chicago, Indiana, that became fully self-supporting within a year. More church-planting initiatives are now underway at FaithWorld.

In 2007 the English-only ministry at FaithWorld merged with a Spanish-only ministry formerly known as *Centro de Restauración Familiar* (Family Restoration Center), a ministry led by Pastor Albert Guerrero, brother-in-law of Pastor Daniel Cruz. Together, they are

---

[48]Rey Martínez, interview with author, January 21, 2010.
[49]Orlando E. Costas, *The Integrity of Mission: The Inner Life and Outreach of the Church* (New York: Harper & Row, 1979), p. 14.

able to accommodate the needs of multiple generations of Latinos in a nontraditional setting. Besides the Adopt-a-Block program and a vibrant children's ministry, a key to the success of FaithWorld is the emphasis placed on relationship building and personal development programs that are gender and age specific. Elite, the women's ministry at FaithWorld directed by Co-Pastor Jennifer Cruz, is dedicated to building healthy Christ-centered self-esteem and confidence among the ladies at FaithWorld, ultimately leading women, wives and mothers to become devoted disciples of Jesus Christ. The men's ministry at Faith-World is called Empowerment and is committed to providing opportunities for husbands and fathers to catch and embrace God's vision for them in homes and a community that lacks positive Christlike male role models. In 2005 FaithWorld established a theatrical productions ministry, which produces "highly professional presentations depicting life's problems, difficulties, and how to triumph in the face of overwhelming challenges."[50]

Many at FaithWorld would agree that Uprise, a dynamic and creative youth ministry, has been crucial to the church's success. Uprise is led by Pastor Eddie Leon and attracts almost three hundred teens each Friday night for a time of fun, praise and celebration. But at the core of every gathering is a challenge to make and keep a commitment to the lordship of Jesus Christ in every area of their lives. Most of the teens at Uprise do not have parents who attend FaithWorld. Instead, they come at the invitation of other teens. Some even come from neighboring Hispanic churches that are perceived by teens as legalistic and concerned more with outward behavior modification than with inward transformation. These include churches where girls are prohibited from wearing makeup and anything but a dress to church services and boys are frowned upon for wearing baggy pants and earrings.

Some Latino teens come to FaithWorld not only to escape the legalism of the traditional Hispanic churches in the neighborhood but also because at FaithWorld they can express themselves in music, dance and theater. Pastor Eddie recalls watching teenagers with experience at

---

[50]FaithWorld Family Church, "About FaithWorld," accessed December 31, 2009 <www.faith worldchicago.com/page/about>.

neighboring churches come to Uprise. They are "like people walking in a desert who suddenly find an oasis."[51] Many parents eventually join their children at FaithWorld, especially now that there are Spanish services available. According to Pastor Eddie, "when parents see the transformation in their kids it justifies the sometimes difficult transition." The same is true of the unchurched teens saved at FaithWorld, who are challenged to be a blessing as well as an example to others, including their unsaved parents. As a result of this creative Christ-centered youth ministry many families have made FaithWorld their church home. It is also worth noting that while the congregation in general is approximately 80 percent Latino, closer to 40 percent of those in attendance at youth events are non-Latino. This suggests that creative and culturally relevant ministries among native-born Latinos are more likely to draw even more non-Latinos in the future, especially if they are offered in English!

PEOPLE SITTING IN DARKNESS "HAVE SEEN A GREAT LIGHT"

The cases studies presented in this chapter remind us that there is a growing need for churches that recognize the unique challenges facing working-class and poor Latinos living in at-risk neighborhoods across the United States. Like children of immigrants before them, the challenges faced by second-generation Hispanic children, teens and young adults are not new. They must deal with high dropout, poverty and delinquency rates, as well as the allure of substance abuse and gangs.

Experts at the National Youth Gang Center (NYGC) remind us that Hispanic youth are especially vulnerable to these so-called traps. For example, the NYGC reported that in 2009 there were 788,000 active gang members in the United States. Approximately 49 percent were Hispanic, 35 percent were African American, and 9 percent were white. Nearly one-third of all gang members were between the ages of thirteen and seventeen. This suggests that somewhere around 130,000 active gang members under the age of seventeen were Hispanic.[52]

---

[51]Eddie Leon, interview with author, May 23, 2007.
[52]National Youth Gang Center, "*National Youth Gang Survey Analysis*," accessed August 1, 2010 <www.nationalgangcenter.gov/Survey-Analysis>.

Scholars insist that "once the cycle of poverty and violence begins in the life of a young Latino/a, it is difficult to break the cycle in subsequent generations."[53]

These ubiquitous urban challenges lead Harold Recinos to argue that Latinos "know what it means to live in a social reality structured in terms of suffering, violence and death." Nevertheless, he correctly insists that the church will find Jesus in our world today by looking at the barrio where poor, rejected and socially and politically oppressed people follow and proclaim "the carpenter from Nazareth to the universal church."[54] It is precisely in the barrio, where the seemingly endless cycle of poverty, despair, violence and death plagues many Latinos, that Jesus is found at Victory Outreach International, Praise Chapel Christian Fellowship and New Harvest Christian Fellowship, three church-planting movements making a difference in the lives of "those who sat in darkness and . . . the shadow of death" (Mt 4:16).

The case studies presented in this chapter also remind us that Hispanic churches, particularly those that target native-born English-dominant Latinos, are uniquely positioned to be the primary proponents of "multicultural America's future."[55] Missionally, churches like those highlighted in this chapter stand well-situated to embrace the evangelistic challenge of creating ethnically and racially diverse churches based on "the understanding that God created human beings to express a multiplicity of languages, lifestyles, and ways of thinking and acting in the world."[56] To that end, the churches highlighted in this chapter prefer to describe themselves as "multiethnic, predominately Hispanic churches." Juan Francisco Martínez has noted, "a church that identifies itself as Latino will generally have little impact among people who have limited identification with Latino culture."[57] Perhaps more importantly, these churches are embracing the opportunity "to teach

---

[53]Johnson-Mondragón, *Pathways for Hope and Faith*, p. 175.
[54]Harold J. Recinos, *Who Comes in the Name of the Lord? Jesus at the Margins* (Nashville: Abingdon, 1997), p. 12.
[55]Ed Morales, *Living in Spanglish: The Search for Latino Identity in America* (New York: St. Martin's Press, 2002), p. 9.
[56]Harold J. Recinos, *Good News from the Barrio: Prophetic Witness for the Church* (Louisville, Ky.: Westminster John Knox, 2006), p. 107.
[57]Martínez, *Walk with the People*, p. 66.

kingdom values that transcend culture and society" to their children and teens, especially to those coping with life at the margins of U.S. society in at-risk underserved neighborhoods. They do so by demonstrating in word and deed that the kingdom of God is superior to any human culture or society. In this way they are forming "young people to be Christians with a worldwide vision, not just with a Latino or a U.S. mindset."[58] Furthermore, as they challenge the socially constructed barriers that keep us apart they rehearse before a divided world the multinational, multiethnic and multilingual celebration envisioned in Revelation 7:9-10.

> After this I looked, and there was a great multitude that no one could count, from every nation, from all tribes and peoples and languages, standing before the throne and before the Lamb, robed in white, with palm branches in their hands. They cried out in a loud voice, saying, "Salvation belongs to our God who is seated on the throne, and to the Lamb!"

---

[58]Juan Francisco Martínez, *Los Evangélicos: Portraits of Latino Protestantism in the United States*, ed. Juan F. Martínez and Lindy Scott (Eugene, Ore.: Wipf and Stock, 2009), p. 14.

GOOD NEWS AND
GOOD WORKS IN THE BARRIO

You know the message he sent to the people of Israel,

preaching peace by Jesus Christ—he is Lord of all. That message

spread throughout Judea, beginning in Galilee after the baptism that John

announced: how God anointed Jesus of Nazareth with the Holy Spirit

and with power; how he went about doing good and healing all who

were oppressed by the devil, for God was with him.

ACTS 10:36-38

THE PHENOMENAL SUCCESS OF CHURCHES like Victory Outreach, Praise Chapel and New Harvest Christian Fellowship reveals a painful reality. Below the small but growing number of middle-class Hispanics lies a much larger group, "the Hispanic underclass." Instead of thriving in their pursuit of the American dream, this group is quickly filling the ranks of the "working poor," severely impoverished people trapped in urban barrios.[1] Demographic data presented in chapter one suggests a strong correlation between the low socioeconomic status of the growing Hispanic underclass, lower levels of educational attainment and the undocumented status of many Latino immigrants. Low income levels associated with limited parental education often leave Latino parents

---

[1]Albert M. Camarillo and Frank Bonilla, "Hispanics in a Multicultural Society: A New American Dilemma?" in *America Becoming: Racial Trends and Their Consequences*, ed. Neil J. Smelzer, William J. Wilson and Faith Mitchell (Washington, D.C.: National Academy Press, 2001), p. 131.

with few options other than living in inner-city barrios where violence, drugs and inferior schools are the norm.[2] This reality highlights the desperate need for churches that not only preach good news, but that are also committed to good works, especially relief, development and social justice.

In the passage above, a reluctant apostle Peter reminds Cornelius that Jesus Christ, the Lord of all, did not "just" preach peace, he also "went about doing good and healing all who were oppressed by the devil" (Acts 10:36-38). Similarly, many Hispanic leaders are reminding the church that in the twenty-first century the real challenge is not just to speak the truth; "The real challenge is to live the truth! As Christians we are called to incarnate the Gospel, to live a life informed by the cross."[3] Marc Rivera, senior pastor at Primitive Christian Church in Manhattan, agrees. Hispanic church leaders "must understand how the power of the Gospel extends beyond the cross." He correctly observes that "the gospel not only saves us for an eternal rest in heaven; it saves us to live an abundant life on earth. It also saves us to be agents of change for the context in which we live as we penetrate the society."[4]

THE NEED FOR HOLISTIC MINISTRY

Nearly two decades ago, Professor Manuel Ortiz sought to convince church leaders that the Hispanic community in the United States presented "a formidable challenge for those committed to evangelism and holistic ministry."[5] Ortiz observed that a growing number of second-generation Latinos had few real prospects of escaping their virtually complete lower- and working-class status.[6] Little has changed in the past twenty years. Latinos continue to have the nation's highest high

---

[2]Ken Johnson-Mondragón, ed., *Pathways for Hope and Faith Among Hispanic Teens: Pastoral Reflections and Strategies Inspired by the National Study of Youth and Religion* (Stockton, Calif.: Instituto Fe y Vida, 2007), p. 165.

[3]Eldín Villafañe, *Beyond Cheap Grace: A Call to Radical Discipleship, Incarnation and Justice* (Grand Rapids: Eerdmans, 2006), p. 4.

[4]Marc Rivera, interview with author, December 8, 2009.

[5]Manuel Ortiz, *The Hispanic Challenge: Opportunities Confronting the Church* (Downers Grove, Ill.: InterVarsity Press, 1993), p. 37.

[6]Ibid., pp. 30-37.

school dropout rate, highest unemployment rate, lowest median income for both men and women, and with few exceptions are among the most likely Americans to live in poverty.

More recently, Professor Daniel Sánchez has observed that the physical, psychosocial and spiritual needs of poor and working-class Latinos continue to represent a "formidable challenge" for churches in the barrio.[7] Clearly one of the greatest challenges facing Hispanic evangelical churches in impoverished urban barrios is the need to embrace "holistic" approaches to ministry patterned after that of Jesus Christ and the early church. Professor Eldín Villafañe agrees: "The brokenness of society (so visible in the barrios and ghettos of our cities), the scriptural missional mandate, and the Spirit's love constrains us to feed the hungry, visit the sick and the prisoners, shelter the homeless and poor—to express God's love in social concerns."[8]

Historically, many Hispanic churches in the United States have successfully penetrated their neighborhoods through the preaching of the gospel accompanied by "mercy ministries," usually referred to as *benevolencia*, consisting of clothes closets, food pantries and emergency financial assistance to needy families. In the case studies that follow, social concern is not only expressed through *benevolencia*, that is, through efforts to provide immediate "relief" for the needy; it is also expressed through "development," efforts to educate and equip people to address and meet their own needs. Some even engage in efforts to change the social and economic structures that create the needs in the first place. For some Hispanic church leaders, these activities and commitments fall outside of what is usually deemed the responsibility and purpose of the local church. Therefore, in the following pages I will briefly outline a biblical paradigm for a more "holistic approach" to ministry. This will be followed by an examination of holistic ministries in several Hispanic churches serving at-risk neighborhoods in cities across the United States.

---

[7]Daniel R. Sánchez, *Hispanic Realities Impacting America: Implications for Evangelism & Missions* (Fort Worth, Tex.: Church Starting Network, 2006), p. 93.

[8]Eldín Villafañe, *Seek the Peace of the City: Reflections on Urban Ministry* (Grand Rapids: Eerdmans, 1995), p. 14.

WHAT IS HOLISTIC MINISTRY?

What exactly do we mean when we affirm that mission and ministry in at-risk Latino communities must be "holistic"? If we listen to missionaries and church leaders working in at-risk and underserved communities at home and abroad, we usually get an impression that the terms "holistic ministry" and "holistic mission" are used to correct what Ron Sider calls "lopsided Christianity," a one-sided understanding of mission that places emphasis on either the vertical or the horizontal dimension of ministry at the expense of the other.[9]

The vertical approach to ministry. Many Christians, including Latino evangelicals, inspired by the Great Commission texts in the New Testament (e.g., Mt 28:18-20; Lk 24:46-47; Acts 1:8) have concluded that the most important tasks entrusted to Christians include preaching the gospel, making and nurturing disciples, and planting indigenous reproducing churches. Ron Sider observes, "they are strong on personal evangelism but with little or no passion for justice for the poor and liberation for the oppressed."[10] The focus of this so-called vertical approach is on life after death, on preparing people to stand confidently in Christ before God on Judgment Day. The assumption is that the world is like a slowly sinking ship, and the objective is to convince the passengers of that fact and get them into the lifeboats (i.e., the church) *tan pronto que sea posible* (as soon as possible).

The horizontal approach to ministry. Others are inspired by Jesus' inaugural sermon (Lk 4:16-21), as well as his public ministry (e.g., Lk 7:18-23) and his call for social responsibility (e.g., Mt 25:31-46; Lk 10:25-37). They have concluded that the most important tasks entrusted to Christians include engaging in social action and social justice. The focus of this so-called horizontal approach is on life before death, on "acting justly and loving mercy" (Mic 6:8). The unspoken assumption is that people need bread *for* life before they will ever be concerned about the Bread *of* Life.

In *Good News and Good Works*, Sider has sadly observed that "each

---

[9]Ronald J. Sider, *Good News and Good Works: A Theology for the Whole Gospel* (Grand Rapids: Baker, 1999), p. 26.
[10]Ibid., p. 16.

group uses the other's one-sidedness to justify its own continuing lack of balance."[11] In response to lopsided Christianity, we need a biblical perspective that inseparably interrelates and intertwines evangelism and social responsibility (i.e., relief, development and structural change) without equating or confusing the one with the other. We need to articulate a biblical perspective that challenges the false dichotomy between evangelism and social responsibility.

THE EXAMPLE OF JESUS

In 1974, at the first International Congress on World Evangelization in Lausanne, John Stott correctly observed that "the mission of the church arises from the mission of God."[12] Therefore, in our search for a remedy to lopsided Christianity, we need to look once again at the example of Jesus Christ, where the mission of God is seen most clearly.

The earliest interpretations of Jesus' life and ministry identify him as the one that Moses predicted would one day come to deliver Israel from bondage. In Acts 3:22, Peter reminds the audience in Herod's temple of the prophecy found in Deuteronomy 18:15, where Moses said, "The Lord your God will raise up for you from your own people a prophet like me. You must listen to whatever he tells you." In Acts 7:37, Stephen quotes from the same passage when he is preaching before the Sanhedrin. And the apostle Philip seems to be referring to the same text in John 1:45 when he tells Nathanael, "We have found him about whom Moses in the law and also the prophets wrote, Jesus son of Joseph from Nazareth." These early statements about the mission of Jesus raise the following question, "Where did the early church get the idea that Jesus was a second Moses?" The answer is obvious. They watched Jesus and listened to his preaching. Here it is instructive to return to Jesus' so-called Nazareth Manifesto in Luke 4:16-21:

> When he came to Nazareth, where he had been brought up, he went to the synagogue on the sabbath day, as was his custom. He stood up to read, and the scroll of the prophet Isaiah was given to him. He unrolled

---

[11]Ibid., p. 17.
[12]J. D. Douglas, ed., *Let the Earth Hear His Voice: International Congress on World Evangelization, Lausanne, Switzerland* (Minneapolis: World Wide Publications, 1975), pp. 66-67.

the scroll and found the place where it was written:

"The Spirit of the Lord is upon me,
>   because he has anointed me
>   to bring good news to the poor.
> He has sent me to proclaim release to the captives
>   and recovery of sight to the blind,
>   to let the oppressed go free,
> to proclaim the year of the Lord's favor."

And he rolled up the scroll, gave it back to the attendant, and sat down. The eyes of all in the synagogue were fixed on him. Then he began to say to them, "Today this scripture has been fulfilled in your hearing."

Reminiscent of Moses, Jesus apparently understood that he had been sent by God to initiate a "new exodus" where freedom would be proclaimed for the prisoners and release proclaimed for the oppressed. So it is not surprising that the Gospels are filled with allusions to the exodus. It also becomes clear why Peter, Stephen and Philip refer to Jesus as the "second Moses." If Christopher Wright is correct when he asserts that the exodus "stands as a paradigmatic and highly repeatable model for the way God wishes to act in the world," then the exodus is an indispensable lens through which we understand Jesus' inaugural sermon in Nazareth as well as his and our ministry.[13]

THE EXODUS: A CASE STUDY IN HOLISTIC MINISTRY

If Jesus understood that his mission was analogous to that of Moses, we must ask ourselves a series of questions. First, why did God deliver Israel from Egypt? Second, what do the exodus narratives reveal about the mission of the church? And finally, what does all this have to say about the relationship between evangelism and social responsibility?

The rationale for the exodus is stated clearly throughout the narrative. In Exodus 3:9-10 the Lord tells Moses, "The cry of the Israelites has now come to me; I have also seen how the Egyptians oppress them.

---

[13]Christopher J. H. Wright, *The Mission of God: Unlocking the Bible's Grand Narrative* (Downers Grove, Ill.: InterVarsity Press, 2006), p. 274.

So come, I will send you to Pharaoh to bring my people, the Israelites, out of Egypt." Observe carefully that the Lord is liberating Israel *from* misery, suffering and oppression. However, two verses later the Lord explains that Israel is being liberated *for* something: worship. He says, "I will be with you; and this shall be the sign for you that it is I who sent you: when you have brought the people out of Egypt, you shall worship God on this mountain" (Ex 3:12). In Exodus 6:6-7, the Lord reiterates the "holistic" rationale for the exodus.

> Say therefore to the Israelites, "I am the LORD, and I will free you from the burdens of the Egyptians and deliver you from slavery to them. I will redeem you with an outstretched arm and with mighty acts of judgment. I will take you as my people, and I will be your God. You shall know that I am the LORD your God, who has freed you from the burdens of the Egyptians."

Here again the Lord reminds Moses that Israel is being redeemed in order to know him and become his people, his servants. After Israel is delivered *from* the hands of the Egyptians, we are told in Exodus 14:31, "Israel saw the great work that the LORD did against the Egyptians. So the people feared the LORD and believed in the LORD and in his servant Moses." Clearly the exodus reveals God's desire to liberate Israel *for* obedience, worship and service to him as their one true God. Unfortunately, the Old Testament also reveals the devastating consequences endured by Israel when she forgot why she was liberated.

The Scriptures remind us that if people are only liberated *from* oppression and not also *for* devotion and service to God, they inevitably become oppressors. Two examples will bear this out. In Leviticus 19:33-34, Israel is commanded to love and care for the aliens who live among them in the Promised Land. But two generations later Boaz informs Ruth the Moabitess that he has given orders to the men not to harm her. If these men had remembered how their ancestors were treated when they lived as aliens in Egypt, this command would have been unnecessary. Centuries later, in the book of Amos, the Lord's judgment is against those he brought "up out of the land of Egypt" (Amos 2:10). They had become like Egyptians, denying justice to the needy, poor and afflicted (Amos 2:6-7). The oppressed had become oppressors. This is the inevitable result of only liberating people *from* oppression and not *for* devotion and service to the God of Moses and Jesus.

Unfortunately, parallels can be found among Latinos as well. For example, in 2002 the largest national survey of Latinos reported that "An overwhelming majority of Latinos [83%] report that Latinos discriminating against other Latinos is a problem, including almost half [48%] who feel that this is a major problem." The Pew study found that Latinos most often attribute this type of discrimination against other Latinos to different socioeconomic and education levels. Thirty-four percent believe that Latinos discriminate against one another based on their country of origin.[14] This phenomenon has been documented most closely in the area of hiring and promotion, where it is referred to as the so-called elephant in the room. Experts note that "skin color, social status and accent are all underlying prejudices that Hispanic employers may consider in Hispanic job applicants."[15] This suggests that in many instances upwardly mobile Latinos (i.e., Hispanic employers) have forgotten their historical roots as vulnerable immigrants or the children of immigrants. Instead, they discriminate against and sometimes even exploit other Hispanics. Undocumented day laborers and those providing domestic services are among the most vulnerable. Thus experts believe that Latinos will increasingly be both "victims and perpetrators of employment discrimination, including Hispanic-on-Hispanic discrimination."[16]

In a brief article titled "Race Discrimination within the Latino Community," Carlos Flores insists that Latino leaders must acknowledge that discrimination and racism exist among our people; we are not color blind.[17] Growing numbers of our people need to be liberated *from* discriminatory practices and exploitation in housing, education, employment, social work, medicine and the criminal justice system. But

---

[14]Pew Hispanic Center and Kaiser Family Foundation, "2002 National Survey of Latinos" (Washington, D.C.: Pew Hispanic Center, December 2002), p. 72.

[15]Workforce Languages Services, "In Hiring, Hispanics Discriminate Against Other Hispanics" (Chicago, Ill.: Workforce Language Services, June 25, 2009).

[16]Enrique Schaerer, "Intragroup Discrimination," *Berkeley Electronic Press* (October 18, 2008), p. 26.

[17]Carlos Flores, "Race Discrimination within the Latino Community," *Diálogo, Center for Latino Research DePaul University* 5 (Winter/Spring 2001): 30-32.

we must also recognize that unless they are liberated *for* devotion and service to the God of Moses and our Lord Jesus Christ, many of today's oppressed Latinos will become tomorrow's oppressors.

AVOIDING LOPSIDED CHRISTIANITY

So what does the exodus suggest about the relationship between social responsibility and evangelism? Socially conscious followers of Christ must recognize that social responsibility and evangelism are inseparable partners, working together like the blades in a pair of scissors.[18] In the case of the exodus, social responsibility (i.e., divine liberation from misery, suffering and oppression at the hands of the Egyptians) was a *bridge* to evangelism. It led to the formation of a people dedicated to be a "priestly kingdom and a holy nation" (Ex 19:3-8). As we will see in the case studies that follow, that is often still the case. However, Jesus' encounter with the rich ruler (Lk 18:22) and Zacchaeus the tax collector (Lk 19:8) remind us that social responsibility is also a divinely anticipated *consequence* of evangelism. And of course social responsibility also *validates* the preaching of the good news. As Christopher Wright observes, "Mission may not always begin with evangelism. But mission that does not ultimately include declaring the Word and the name of Christ, the call to repentance, and faith and obedience has not completed its task. It is defective, not holistic mission."[19] This is the same conclusion Ray Bakke comes to as he reflects on Philip's mission among the despised Samaritans. "Hear me when I say, *Evangelism must be at the front line of ministry if it is to have integrity with the poorest and most despised peoples of our planet at all times and in every place!* Through evangelism the early church put its arms around a previously despised people, baptized them and welcomed them into the church."[20]

Finally, we must recall that most of those liberated *from* Egyptian oppression and injustice were destined to perish in the wilderness rather than enter the Promised Land because they failed to honor and serve

---

[18]John Stott, ed., *Making Christ Known: Historic Mission Documents from the Lausanne Movement, 1974-1989* (Grand Rapids: Eerdmans, 1996), pp. 181-82.

[19]Wright, *The Mission of God*, p. 319.

[20]Ray Bakke, *A Theology as Big as the City* (Downers Grove, Ill.: InterVarsity Press, 1997), p. 142.

the God who liberated them. Likewise Jesus, the "Second Moses," indicated that the oppressed as well as those who oppress them must not sin anymore. Instead they must put their trust in him as Lord and Savior, or they too would die in their sins (Jn 5:14; 8:24). Unfortunately, this will not happen simply by Christians showing mercy and doing justice. Neither will it happen by preaching the gospel alone. Like Jesus, we too must both go around "doing good" (Acts 10:38) and preach the good news of Jesus (Mk 1:15). As Ron Sider has noted, for the sake of all of those who still live in Egypt both here and abroad, the world needs "Christians so in love with Jesus Christ that they lead scores of people to accept him as personal Savior and Lord—and so sensitive to the cry of the poor and oppressed that they work vigorously for justice, peace and freedom."[21] The Hispanic churches highlighted in the case studies that follow are filled with just such people.

THE NEED FOR HOLISTIC MINISTRY IN THE BARRIO

In the modern classic *Christ Outside the Gate,* the late Orlando Costas identified the barrio as *the* place where holistic mission and ministry would give witness to the kingdom of God in the United States.

> Evangelization in the United States means bearing witness in the power of the Spirit to the new world that God has promised in Jesus Christ. Such a witness can only be given from within situations where the signs of that new world are present, where love and freedom, justice and peace are being experienced—even if in small and limited ways. And the one place where this is happening is in *the other* American church—the church of the disfranchised racial minorities, which has been living in and witnessing from the underside of American history.[22]

Fortunately, the churches highlighted in this chapter combine their historic commitment to the Great Commission with an equally strong commitment to compassion ministries and social justice, evident in many social services offered in what Costas calls "the *other* American church."

---

[21]Sider, *Good News and Good Works,* p. 18.
[22]Orlando E. Costas, *Christ Outside the Gate: Mission Beyond Christendom* (Maryknoll, N.Y.: Orbis, 1982), p. 185.

THEOLOGICAL OBSTACLES TO HOLISTIC MINISTRY IN THE BARRIO

Nevertheless, not all Hispanic church leaders are convinced of the inseparable relationship between evangelism and social responsibility. Several theological assumptions account for the reluctance of many to embrace more holistic approaches to ministry. Reflecting on his survey of urban Hispanic churches, Harvie Conn observed that some Hispanic pastors and churches confine Christian discipleship to personal piety and the "verbal" proclamation of the gospel. They envision the church at war against the secularizing and corrupting influences of *el mundo* (the world), which can have the effect of minimizing "the role of the church in society as an agent of justice, freedom, and peace." Instead, the world is seen and approached "as a dying place," and social responsibility beyond benevolence is seen as a "fruitless waste of time." Conn observes that in many instances these "negative eschatological views" are imported from the countries of origin in Latin America where evangelical churches have historically been marginalized and forced into a defensive posture.[23]

Harold Recinos believes that another source of resistance to holistic ministry is a truncated view of evangelism. He contends that the "contemporary church misunderstands evangelism when it simply equates it with personal evangelism and church growth instead of following Jesus. Evangelism should keep us close to human suffering for the purpose of discerning and responding to the loving God who frees us from the values of a divided cultural order."[24]

Eldín Villafañe suggests that the reluctance to embrace a more holistic approach to ministry can be traced to a truncated view of Christian spirituality. He reminds us that holistic ministry flows out of a "holistic spirituality" patterned after the ministry of Jesus Christ. He and others urge the church to acknowledge "that an authentic and relevant spirituality must be wholistic, responding to both the vertical and horizontal dimensions of life. The inclusion of the social dimension in

---

[23]Harvie Conn, *The American City and the Evangelical Church: A Historical Overview* (Grand Rapids: Baker Academic 1994), pp. 169-70.
[24]Harold J. Recinos, *Good News from the Barrio: Prophetic Witness for the Church* (Louisville, Ky.: Westminster John Knox, 2006), p. 33.

a *redefinition* of spirituality is the missing ingredient of contemporary evangelical spirituality."[25] More recently Villafañe has argued that authentic spirituality requires "a mind informed by the cross."[26] In other words, "the cross demands action from us to oppose the conditions that lead to death and suffering in our world."[27] This is the same argument made so passionately by Richard Stearns, president of World Vision U.S., in his book *The Hole in Our Gospel*.[28]

Fortunately, the churches highlighted in this study have learned that in order to reach the Hispanic community with the life-transforming power of the gospel they too must "proclaim release to the captives and recovery of sight to the blind, [and] let the oppressed go free." In the process they build trust and relationships through which those "living in the shadow of death" become open to "the year of the Lord's favor" (Lk 4:18-19).

New Life Covenant Ministries, Chicago, Illinois

In 2000, before agreeing to become the new senior pastor at *Templo Cristiano Palestina*, Wilfredo De Jesús proposed a fundamental shift in the church's traditional approach to ministry. While assuring the congregation that he would continue to serve every member of the church, Pastor De Jesús insisted that he had been called by God to serve the entire community of Humboldt Park, including hurting people from diverse linguistic and cultural backgrounds.[29] He soon proposed a new name and new vision for the church. *Templo Cristiano Palestina* would soon become New Life Covenant Ministries, "a Christ-like congregation that transforms the community into a NEW LIFE."[30] Initial fears, resistance and reluctance to agree with the proposed changes were mitigated by the unprecedented growth during the next ten years. Today New Life Covenant Ministries offers five services each Sunday in the

---

[25]Villafañe, *Seek the Peace of the City*, p. 12.

[26]Villafañe, *Beyond Cheap Grace*, p. 7.

[27]Luis Pedraja, *Jesus Is My Uncle: Christology from a Hispanic Perspective* (Nashville: Abingdon, 1999), p. 70.

[28]Richard Stearns, *The Hole in Our Gospel* (Nashville: Thomas Nelson, 2010).

[29]Wilfredo De Jesús, interview with author, May 23, 2008.

[30]New Life Covenant Ministries. "Mission and Vision," accessed May 16, 2008 <www.mynewlife.org/Content.aspx?content_id=9545&site_id=10087>.

auditorium at Roberto Clemente High School, where the combined attendance averages over five thousand per weekend.

Curious observers trying to understand the phenomenal success at New Life Covenant Ministries (NLCM) will often hear people associated with the church repeat the logo found on its walls, website and in all of its literature: "A Church for the Hurting."[31] Pastor Wilfredo De Jesús has been instrumental in the development of several nonprofit faith-based organizations that validate this claim and help explain the unprecedented growth experienced over the past ten years. In 1998 New Life Family Services, a nonprofit agency, was incorporated as an extension of the church. Until 2007, when New Life Family Services came under the umbrella of the church's new Chicago Dream Center, it operated a homeless shelter for women with children as well as an after school program.

Modeled after the Los Angeles Dream Center,[32] the Chicago Dream Center (CDC) is a nonprofit organization that provides hope and services for meeting both tangible and spiritual needs. The CDC reaches out to hurting men, women and children, including the homeless, drug addicts, prostitutes and ex-convicts by providing food and clothing, shelter for homeless and abused women, job skills and spiritual guidance.

Several creative and holistic ministries of the CDC deserve to be mentioned here. New Life for Women Outreach targets women living and working on the streets that have been destroyed by gangs, drugs and alcohol. Not only is the gospel of Jesus Christ shared with these women, they are also informed about the recovery program that is offered to those ready to begin a new life. The Dream Center for Women is a fifteen month faith-based program providing hope and residential care for women suffering from drug addition, alcoholism and any other life-controlling issues. The Dream Center for Women provides a protective and nurturing environment where women are exposed to the

---

[31]Ibid.

[32]For the history and description of the Dream Center L.A., see Matthew Barnett, *The Church That Never Sleeps* (New York: Thomas Nelson, 2000) as well as their website: <http://dream center.org/>.

life-transforming power of Christ revealed in the Bible and through the power of the Holy Spirit.[33]

To meet the immediate felt needs in the neighborhood, other outreach ministries of NLCM include Manna 4 Life, a food pantry that distributes groceries to families in the community. A program called Battle assists women struggling in abusive relationships by providing shelter as well as hope and encouragement through Christ as they seek legal assistance in difficult and dangerous circumstances. Gangs to Grace is a ministry effective in reaching gang members for Christ. Foundation Family Ministry equips couples, parents and children to work as one in the body of Christ by building firm and healthy foundations needed for setting priorities, communicating and making financial decisions as a family. Another program, Kingdom Economic$, empowers families by helping them to implement hidden biblical principles that are designed to lead them towards financial freedom. With the exception of River of Life Women's Shelter, which is funded by the Chicago Department of Human Services, programs and ministries offered at the CDC and NLCM are funded by the church, proving that it is indeed "a church for the hurting."[34]

Templo Calvario, Santa Ana, California

On the West Coast, *Templo Calvario* is also redefining the relationship between preaching good news and doing good works in an at-risk and underserved neighborhood in southern California where 80 percent of the population is Hispanic and 50 percent are foreign born. In the past thirty years Senior Pastor Daniel de Leon has helped turn a small Spanish-speaking immigrant congregation into one of the largest multigenerational and multilingual Hispanic churches in the United States, with more than six thousand members.

In 2003, under the leadership of Pastor de Leon's bother Lee, *Templo Calvario* launched Templo Calvario Community Development Corporation (TCCDC), a nonprofit faith-based organization that op-

---

[33]New Life Covenant Ministries, "Ministries," accessed April 10, 2009 <www.mynewlife.org/Ministries.aspx?site_id=10087>.
[34]Ibid.

erates a daycare program, after school programs, a public charter school as well as numerous economic development initiatives that feed and clothe the poor, provide job training and job placement, and educate and involve young adults in social justice and public policy issues that impact the community.

One of the mottos heard regularly at *Templo Calvario* is *"soy bendecido para bendecir"* ("I am blessed to bless"). More than a motto, it is a conviction that shapes the lives of hundreds of volunteers every week at *Templo Calvario*, where according to Pastor Danny de Leon, "It's the poor helping the poor."[35]

I will highlight three creative and unusually successful initiatives of the TCCDA. The first is *Obras de Amor* (Works of Love), a food bank that monthly distributes fifteen to twenty tons of food to families in need and to more than twenty partner organizations that make up the Kingdom Coalition, a network of community-based and faith-based organizations. The church and its coalition of partners feed more than 900,000 people and give away $10.6 million worth of food, clothing and household items annually.[36]

Through an initiative called *Esperanza Trabajando* (Hope Working), TCCDC serves the court by providing job training and job placement for adjudicated youth. In conjunction with Jobing.com, *Esperanza Trabajando* also provides church members and the community with the most comprehensive listing of employment opportunities throughout Southern California.

To address the need to educate and involve young men and women concerning social justice and public policy issues that impact their community, TCCDC started Acts of Compassion Transforming Society (ACTS). Through ACTS a young generation of leaders is being nurtured to act justly, love mercy and walk humbly with their God. They not only seek to educate themselves and others about social issues that impact their community, they are also committed to mobilize others to

---

[35]Drew Dyck, Jon Rising and Joel Kilpatrick, "2007 Models in Innovation: Something from Nothing," *Ministry Today*, accessed April 11, 2009 <www.ministrytodaymag.com/display .php?id=14742>.

[36]Templo Calvario, "Obras de Amor," accessed April 11, 2009 <http://www.templocalvario .com/obras.html>.

serve and stand up for those in need. The organization emerged after a group of young adults from the church traveled to Washington, D.C., in 2007 to support the farm bill sponsored by Bread for the World. Since then the group has committed itself to seek just policies for the poor and in public education, as well as labor and immigration reform, issues that directly affect the members of their church and community.[37]

Whenever possible, rather than use the limited resources and personnel at the church to duplicate social services offered by governmental and nongovernmental agencies, *Templo Calvario* seeks what Pastor Marc Rivera in New York calls "programmatic partnerships." Programmatic partnerships link the congregation's needs with community-based organizations that are already providing the social services needed or that are willing to fund much-needed social programs through the church's nonprofit faith-based entity, TCCDC. "Why use church offerings and tithes to provide a particular [social] service, when we can partner with an agency that is funded to accomplish that goal," asks Pastor Rivera. He insists that while the immediate goal of several programs offered by churches like his and those targeted in this study is to respond to real and felt needs within the Hispanic community, the net result is that "the kingdom of God is being built in the institutions that partner with us and in the people we serve."[38]

Good News and Good Works in San Antonio, Texas

On the Southside of San Antonio, Texas, two congregations are having a huge influence on their community—South San Filadelfia Church and *Vida Abundante*. South San Filadelfia Church (SSFC) is doing this primarily through goodwill events that give neighbors a peak into the heart of this multigenerational, multilingual Southern Baptist church that has grown from 150 members in 2002 to more than 900 members in 2009.[39] Led by Senior Pastor Victor Rodríguez, the church sponsors several well-advertised neighborhood events including free biannual health clinics, school supply giveaways in the fall, a Halloween-

---

[37]Templo Calvario, "ACTS," accessed April 11, 2009 <www.acts-online.us/About_Us.html>.
[38]Marc Rivera, interview with author, April 3, 2009.
[39]A description and analysis of the growth of this church is described in chapter two.

alternative block party as well as an annual Father's Day car show and motorcycle blessing, to name just a few.

The unique thing about the goodwill events at SSFC is that each event is strategically evangelistic. Pastor Rodríguez and his leadership team prayerfully select and plan each event with the community's felt and deeper spiritual needs in mind. Committed to excellence, they advertize each event well. On the day of the event, staff and ministry leaders are present and visible serving as hosts and intentionally building relationships. Other volunteers are careful to get accurate contact information for every participant. This invaluable information is then carefully inputted into a growing database of individuals and households that have had contact with the church. Soon after an event, bilingual teams are sent to follow up and share information about ongoing programs and ministries offered at SSFC. Next, the appropriate cell group is given the responsibility of inviting guests to an intimate neighborhood event like a backyard BBQ, where relationships are nurtured and every opportunity is made to demonstrate a sincere concern for the material and spiritual needs of the group's neighbors.[40]

In the past three years SSFC has also started boys' and girls' soccer and T-ball leagues and opened a neighborhood playground. Each was designed to offer family-friendly and healthy recreational opportunities for children in the barrio that put neighbors in contact with the church staff and members in a nonthreatening setting, furthering SSFC's visibility and credibility on the Southside of San Antonio.[41]

Not far from SSFC, *Vida Abundante* is also making a significant impact on its neighborhood on the Southside of San Antonio. Senior Pastor Eliezer Bonilla insists that if someone is interested in how *Vida Abundante* grew from 350 to more than 2,000 members in six years, he points to the historic decision to abandon bilingual services for separate Spanish and English services.[42] But he also insists that often overlooked is the critical role of the vibrant cell-group ministry that keeps this

---

[40]Victor Rodríguez, interview with author, July 27, 2008.
[41]Victor Rodríguez, interview with author, June 16, 2009.
[42]See chapter two for more details concerning the rationale and outcome of this decision.

megachurch "relationship driven rather than event driven."[43] More surprising is Pastor Bonilla's conviction that the most successful "social service" offered by *Vida Abundante* is not the food bank that serves over three hundred families per week, but the more than three hundred cell groups that sensitively incarnate the love of God in Christ at the "grassroots level," where church members are intimately aware of the needs of family members, friends, coworkers and neighbors.

At *Vida Abundante* the cell group functions as a team of missionaries as a well as a miniature church, where group leaders have been trained to look at their cell groups with the eyes of an evangelist as well as the eyes of a pastor. With the former, the group leader teaches and models for his or her group the holistic concern of Christ. Like a group of conscientious Christlike social workers, members are on the lookout for individuals and families in distress, both inside and outside of the church. In most cases the cell group can respond immediately to the needs that arise, whether this involves help with groceries, assistance paying the rent or utilities, or a tip and *palanca* (i.e., influence) finding a job. At other times the cell group refers the individual or family to the staff, especially when legal assistance is needed with cases involving family law or immigration law. But the "point-of-contact" for virtually all social services at *Vida Abundante* is the cell group.

Even on Tuesday mornings when more than three hundred families gather each week at the main campus to receive groceries from the church's food bank, several cell groups are strategically meeting simultaneously at the church. Some are there to set up, host and give groceries away to needy families. Others open up their groups to those who are awaiting their turn to receive their weekly ration of food. When volunteers learn of an unmet need, the information is discreetly passed on to a cell-group leader whose group assumes responsibility for addressing the need with the resources readily available among cell-group members. The integral place of the cell group in the life of the church not only decentralizes the "social service" delivery system, it humanizes it as well. This is due to the fact that lay members rather than profes-

---

[43]Eliezer Bonilla, interview with author, June 16, 2009.

sionals are the face of the church to its community, and the reality that people are treated as neighbors and friends rather than clients in a church that strategically combines good news with good works in the context of a small group. Eli Bonilla insists that it all flows from a commitment to be relational.[44]

CONCLUSION

Today, a growing number of Hispanic churches are looking for creative and God-glorifying ways to make a lasting and transforming impact on their neighborhoods. Some, like those highlighted in this chapter, continue to find ways to do just that and in the process address the deeper needs for restoration and reconciliation with God available only through the atoning sacrifice of Christ. At the churches highlighted in this chapter, the Great Commission and great compassion including social justice are inseparable partners as each church extends its ministry into the community. Like other Christians working in at-risk contexts, Hispanic evangelicals address the felt needs of their communities for at least three reasons. Meeting felt needs provides a point of redemptive connection with those who are spiritually lost, it adds credibility to their communication of the gospel, and most importantly, it is commanded by God and demonstrated by Christ.[45]

Evangelical leaders like pastors Wilfredo De Jesús, Daniel de Leon, Marc Rivera, Victor Rodríguez and Eliezer Bonilla are often criticized for preaching a so-called social gospel or for compromising on evangelism. Undeterred, they and their congregations have made a commitment to demonstrate the same broad concern for human need that God consistently demonstrated in the exodus on behalf of Israel and in the ministry of Jesus. In other words, these pastors are convinced that "the scope of our mission must reflect the scope of God's mission, which in turn will match the scale of God's redemptive work."[46]

---

[44]Eliezer Bonilla, interview with author, December 11, 2009.
[45]Craig W. Ellison, "Addressing the Felt Needs of Urban Dwellers," in *Planting and Growing Urban Churches: From Dream to Reality*, ed. Harvie M. Conn (Grand Rapids: Baker, 1997), p. 94.
[46]Wright, *Mission of God*, p. 265.

~~ 5 ~~

THE LOCAL CHURCH
AS ORGANIC SEMINARY

Saul clothed David with his armor; he put a bronze helmet on his
head and clothed him with a coat of mail. David strapped Saul's sword over
the armor, and he tried in vain to walk, for he was not used to them.
Then David said to Saul, "I cannot walk with these; for I am not
used to them." So David removed them. Then he took his staff in
his hand, and chose five smooth stones from the wadi,
and put them in his shepherd's bag, in the pouch;
his sling was in his hand, and he drew near to the Philistine.

1 SAMUEL 17:38-40

SIMILAR TO DAVID IN THE ALL-TOO-FAMILIAR episode in which he killed Goliath the Philistine, many aspiring Hispanic pastors must wrestle with the question of the appropriate weapons or theological training needed to effectively engage the Goliaths that terrorize many at-risk urban barrios in the United States. Modern day giants in urban barrios include grinding poverty; inadequate and unaffordable health-care; underfunded, underachieving and unsafe schools; soaring high school dropout rates; teenage pregnancy; unemployment; crime and gang-infested neighborhoods; broken families; and hopelessness, to name just a few. And these are just the symptoms or consequences of deeper problems such as rebellion and alienation from God and subsequent enslavement to the power of sin and death.

In response to the need for appropriate weapons to take on these giants, Bible colleges, Christian universities and seminaries suggest putting on Saul's armor. That is, they offer denominational or ATS-approved curricula and credentials required of pastors in most denominations serving the dominant group (i.e., non-Hispanic whites). However, a growing number of modern day Hispanic giant killers are being encouraged to rely instead on the training and experience they can acquire at the feet of a pastor in the context of the local church.

This chapter will highlight and analyze contextually appropriate and indefinitely reproducible approaches to leadership development in predominately Hispanic evangelical churches that are successfully reaching native-born Latinos in the United States. One of the outstanding characteristics of the churches targeted in this study is their ability to identify, train and empower indigenous leaders in the context of the local church. By necessity, pastoral leadership development successfully shortcuts the traditional approach that looks to preacher-training schools, Bible colleges, Christian universities or seminaries to provide the church with qualified ministers and pastors.

This chapter will also examine the theological assumptions as well as the socioeconomic and cultural factors that have shaped the ministry paradigms in at-risk and underserved communities where Hispanic pastors have rediscovered the local church as the "organic seminary" par excellence for identifying, training and nurturing indigenous ministers, pastors, church planters and other servant leaders.

LEADERSHIP DEVELOPMENT IN THE BARRIO

One key to the rapid and sometimes phenomenal growth of the churches highlighted in this study is an emphasis on discipleship programs and leadership development in the context of the local church. There are numerous contextual factors that force many urban and inner-city Hispanic churches to bypass the traditional role of Bible colleges, universities and seminaries in most Protestant and evangelical denominations. Many would-be ministers and pastors in these churches do not qualify academically for admission to most institutions that train men and women for ministry. More importantly, family obligations and the ongoing needs of the local Hispanic church will dissuade aspiring leaders from taking anywhere from two to seven years away from the ministry in order to obtain the training and minimum credentials required of ministers and pastors in most denominations. Furthermore, many of the most respected and influential church leaders have followed a process into pastoral leadership that has relied on competencies gained at the level of the local church. Manuel Ortiz describes the historic or "recommended process" for approaching pastoral ministry in most Hispanic churches, including those highlighted in this study:

> The route usually begins by potential leaders proving themselves in the local church while becoming "faithful members." The pastor pays closer attention to these individuals, considers them to be dependable, and entrusts them with additional responsibilities. They may teach, work with youth, lead services, coordinate ministries, and preach periodically. The training takes place while doing ministry, the need for education is triggered by actual hands on involvement. Eventually the mother church formally affirms their calling, ordains them, and establishes an independent ministry for them to lead.[1]

The process outlined above by Manuel Ortiz in 1993 is still normative in many Hispanic communities, where an "entrepreneurial spirit" often drives leadership in Hispanic evangelical churches where would-be pastors are often recognized by their "calling" before they are recognized for their credentials. Indirectly, the so-called recommended process also reveals inherent weaknesses perceived by many Hispanic church leaders in the education and training one receives in many Bible colleges, universities and seminaries, not the least of which is that these institutions do not offer contextually appropriate models of leadership development.

INSTITUTIONAL AND CURRICULAR FACTORS

In a provocative chapter titled "Getting David Out of Saul's Armor," Roger Greenway, Professor Emeritus of World Missiology at Calvin Theological Seminary, makes an invaluable contribution to the dis-

---

[1]Manuel Ortiz, *The Hispanic Challenge: Opportunities Confronting the Church* (Downers Grove, Ill.: InterVarsity Press, 1993), pp. 143-44.

cussion of leadership development in Hispanic churches. He laments that it is unrealistic to expect seminaries to provide the type of training that leadership in urban contexts requires. Such contexts require "training that is biblically based, theologically valid, *and contextualized to urban realities that are marked by ethnic diversity, cultural pluralism, wide educational differences, enormous social and economic problems, and rapid change.*"[2] Greenway is not optimistic concerning the ability of most traditional academic institutions to change and adapt to meet the needs of urban churches like those highlighted in this study. Instead, he prefers to see church leaders "develop new forms of leadership training that are more church- and ministry-based, that build in a simple and straightforward manner on the authoritative Word of God and how it applies to people's lives."[3]

Puerto-Rican born Alvin Padilla, professor and director for the Center for Urban Ministerial Education (CUME) at Gordon-Conwell Theological Seminary, is sympathetic to the sentiments above, but is nonetheless hopeful that ATS-accredited seminaries can make the necessary adjustments. In an insightful chapter titled "Living in the Hyphen: Theological Literacy from an Hispanic American Perspective," Padilla observes that the problem is essentially one of definition: In this case, what constitutes "theological literacy"? Traditional theological institutions define "theological literacy" or competency as "at least a passing knowledge of apologetics, dogmatic and systematic theology, religion and history, biblical and exegetical studies, and worship."[4] Unfortunately, theological literacy or competency seldom includes the ability to effectively apply theological insights gained in the institution to the daily life of the local church. This fundamental weakness in traditional theological education often produces pastors who, in spite of their training and credentials, are perceived as "theo-

---

[2]Roger S. Greenway, "Getting David Out of Saul's Armor," in *The Urban Face of Mission: Ministering the Gospel in a Diverse and Changing World*, ed. Manuel Ortiz and Susan S. Baker (Phillipsburg, N.J.: P & R Publishers, 2002), p. 229.

[3]Ibid., p. 231.

[4]Alvin Padilla, "Living in the Hyphen: Theological Literacy from an Hispanic American Perspective," in *Theological Literacy for the Twenty-First Century*, ed. Rodney L. Petersen with Nancy M. Rourke (Grand Rapids: Eerdmans, 2002), p. 229.

logically *illiterate*" in the eyes of their congregants.[5]

Padilla insists that theological competency in the Hispanic-American context is defined differently than in the dominant group, which most seminaries have in mind as they train men and women for ministry. For example, he argues that the Hispanic context requires competent pastors to have an appreciation of the Hispanic struggle for identity as they live in the hyphen between Latino and American. Here Padilla is informed by what Eldín Villafañe, his colleague at Gordon-Conwell Theological Seminary, refers to as a "triple-consciousness paradigm," the sociocultural dilemma of many native-born Latinos living with a hyphenated identity.[6] They are at once "insiders" and "outsiders" of both identifying ethnic groups (Latino and American), while at the same time experiencing rejection by both.[7] At the level of the local church, sensitivity to life in the hyphen also means that theological competence will include a commitment "to the social struggle of our people," to embrace our "*lucha*, the struggle for survival."[8] Unfortunately, too many institutions assume "church structures and theological traditions which are purely expressions of Western European cultural and theological reflections" that do not reflect the context of Hispanic churches in the United States, especially in at-risk underserved neighborhoods.[9]

Predictably, some church leaders and academics recommend that "urban churches set the academy aside, with everything it entails—degrees, accreditation, Ph.D.s, credit hours and traditional curriculum—and focus relentlessly on the needs of the churches, the skills required for ministry, and the biblical standards for leaders of God's people."[10] Others, including Alvin Padilla and Eldín Villafañe, are cautiously optimistic and offer proposals for "an effective seminary-based urban theological education program" modeled after Gordon

---

[5]Ibid., p. 234.

[6]For a recent discussion on this topic from a Puerto Rican perspective, see Orlando Crespo, *Being Latino in Christ: Finding Wholeness in Your Ethnic Identity* (Downers Grove, Ill.: InterVarsity Press, 2003), pp. 27-39.

[7]Eldín Villafañe, *The Liberating Spirit: Toward an Hispanic American Pentecostal Social Ethic* (Grand Rapids: Eerdmans, 1993), p. 22.

[8]Padilla, "Living in the Hyphen," p. 238.

[9]Ibid., p. 240.

[10]Greenway, "Getting David Out of Saul's Armor," p. 233.

Conwell's Center for Urban Ministerial Education (CUME) in Boston.[11] Initiatives like those at Gordon-Conwell represent promising examples of theological education programs contributing to the Shalom of Hispanic urban neighborhoods.

In their important study titled *Developing Leaders for Urban Ministries*, well-respected seminary professors Edgar J. Elliston and J. Timothy Kaufman argue that traditional theological education programs too often "produce non-functional or dysfunctional ministry candidates."[12] However, unlike those who encourage urban churches to set aside the seminary, Eddie Elliston argues that what happens in the local church "precedes, compliments, supplements and legitimizes what happens in Christian higher education."[13] But as the case studies below will demonstrate, many promising Hispanic leaders are not in a position to take advantage of even the best urban theological education programs like CUME at Gordon-Conwell. Instead, they must rely almost exclusively on the training they receive in the local church.

Among many Hispanic urban pastors, another inherent weakness in Christian higher education is the lack of attention given to character development, spiritual formation and development of ministry skills critical in the Hispanic urban context. Conversely, theological training in the context of the local church usually begins with character development and spiritual formation, followed by the development of necessary skills for ministry. It then concerns itself with imparting knowledge of God and his word informed by the needs of the ministry context.[14]

The case studies that follow describe the leadership development

---

[11]Eldín Villafañe, *Seek the Peace of the City: Reflections on Urban Ministry* (Grand Rapids: Eerdmans, 1995), pp. 77-96. Villafañe describes six essential elements or criteria for evaluating the effectiveness of seminary-based urban theological education programs. These criteria include a clear vision of the program's target constituency, the investment of valuable resources, a holistic curriculum, the blessing of the host community, full integration into the life of the host seminary, and a long-term financial commitment to the program.

[12]Edgar J. Elliston and J. Timothy Kauffman, *Developing Leaders for Urban Ministries*, American University Studies, v. 147 (New York: Peter Lang, 1993), p. 1; Robert W. Ferris, *Renewal in Theological Education: Strategies for Change* (Wheaton, Ill.: The Billy Graham Center, Wheaton College, 1990), pp. 45-126.

[13]Edgar J. Elliston, *Home Grown Leaders* (Pasadena, Calif.: William Carey Library, 1992), p. 4.

[14]Greenway, "Getting David out of Saul's Armor," pp. 234-35.

models of two church-planting movements introduced earlier in this study, Victory Outreach International (VOI) and Praise Chapel Christian Fellowship (PCCF). As we observed earlier in this study, each of these movements has enjoyed remarkable success reaching native-born Latinos in at-risk urban neighborhoods. Led by hundreds of pastors trained almost exclusively in the context of the local church, VOI and PCCF have successfully planted hundreds of healthy and evangelistic churches across the United States in at-risk Hispanic neighborhoods.

THE LOCAL CHURCH AS SEMINARY

One key to the phenomenal growth in church-planting movements like VOI and PCCF is an emphasis on discipleship programs and leadership development in the context of the local church, bypassing the formal theological training required in most Protestant denominations. Several reasons for this are mentioned by leaders in each movement. First, many of their would-be pastors are high school dropouts with criminal records who would not qualify for admission to most traditional training institutions. More importantly, the urgent needs in the local church and the evangelistic fervor in their hearts make taking the time to obtain the training and credentials required of pastors in most denominations an unattractive option. In his study of PCCF, Ron Simpkins observed that for the sake of the kingdom, this pattern had to be broken.

> Too many churches put a cap on those men who feel a call to ministry. A church's traditions, habits and patterns put obstacles in the way of real ministry. The best they can offer is to go off to Bible school and then maybe preach in the distant future. Only the most determined young men and women find their way into the pulpit. The most exciting thing that happened in those early days was when men started to rise up and say, *"I want to preach, I want to be like* [Pastor Mike Neville]."[15]

Similarly, Pastor Sonny Arguinzoni recalls his early efforts to get his young pastors ordained. The problem was that most were former drug

---

[15]Ron Simpkins, *The Harvest Generation: The Story of Praise Chapel* (Huntington Park, Calif.: Mission Global Harvest Press, 1994), p. 26.

addicts who hadn't finished high school and had criminal records. Of the few who were qualified to get into Bible school, many complained, "I don't want to go to school. I'm ready to preach right now. I mean I'm ready to go out right now."[16] According to Pastor Sonny, some of those who did go to Bible college "lost their fire, their enthusiasm and their vision. They got discouraged. Even worse, some got so sophisticated that they were ineffective on the street. They tried to act like all the other preachers. They couldn't identify with the needs of our people anymore."[17]

Biblical injunctions like those found in 1 Timothy 2:12 exclude women from serving as pastors at VOI and PCCF. But women young and old do lead many ministries and programs under the oversight of their pastors. However, wives of pastors are regularly referred to as "co-pastors" and treated with the utmost respect, especially those women gifted at preaching and teaching. It is for this reason that Donna Neville continued to serve as senior pastor of the mother church of PCCF after her husband passed away. But Pastor Donna acknowledges that she is an anomaly at PCCF.[18]

Today qualified Victory Outreach pastors are encouraged to further their education whenever possible; many of them do, earning theological degrees at institutions such as Azusa Pacific, Biola, Dallas Theological Seminary, Fuller Seminary, Hartford Seminary, Gordon-Conwell, Wheaton College and Moody Bible Institute, to mention a few. But young pastors are reminded regularly that "education does not anoint you for ministry." That is the job of the Holy Spirit. Proof of their anointing by God himself is their ability to boldly take the gospel into dangerous inner-city streets, win hundreds of broken lives to Christ and start new churches.[19]

While most Victory Outreach churches tend to be between one hundred and three hundred members, some are quite large. When questioned about the unusual success enjoyed by Rick Alanis and Ed

---

[16]Sonny Arguinzoni, *Internalizing the Vision* (San Dimas, Calif.: Vision Multimedia, 1995), pp. 57-58.

[17]Ibid., p. 58.

[18]Donna Neville, interview with author, November 22, 2009.

[19]Arguinzoni, *Internalizing the Vision*, pp. 58-59.

Morales, pastors of thousand-plus member VOI churches in San Bernardino and San Jose respectively, Sonny Arguinzoni commented that they were naturally bright and talented individuals, who could have succeeded in any endeavor if sinful choices and bad habits as young men had not disqualified them. Nevertheless, their dedication to the God-given vision of VOI and loyalty to Pastor Sonny, their teacher, mentor and friend, allowed each pastor to develop the character and acquire the skills and knowledge that has made them role models throughout the movement.[20]

Today, decades after these two movements were born in the barrio, men, women and married couples who express a desire to become rehab home directors, evangelists, church planters or pastors are encouraged to start and lead home Bible study groups, targeting their own unchurched neighborhoods, friends and family members. Since most of the group leaders were first introduced to Christ through one of these informal Bible study and prayer groups, they know firsthand that one of the most important "credentials" needed for effective ministry is unswerving faith in the power of God to break the cycle of sin, suffering and death. They have also learned through personal experience in these small groups that the key to unleashing this transforming power is fervent prayer in Jesus' name and the power of the Holy Spirit. Finally, they have learned that a sincere personal testimony is indispensable for validating their message in the barrio, where hopelessness reigns generation after generation in broken and dysfunctional homes. Small groups also provide would-be church planters and pastors with opportunities to develop their preaching and pastoral skills under the direction and supervision of the local pastor.[21]

As Bible study leaders develop their skills at preaching, intercessory prayer and leading worship in the context of home Bible study groups, those who demonstrate unique giftedness, faithfulness and commitment to the vision of the pastor are given opportunities to lead at the congregational level, where their lives serve as powerful examples to motivate others to follow the indefinitely reproducible pattern of lead-

---

[20]Sonny Arguinzoni, interview with author, May 10, 2007.
[21]Ibid.

ership development in the context of the local church. The entire process is under the supervision of the local pastor, who like the apostle Paul continually has his or her eyes open for those like Timothy and Priscilla who have proven themselves. Local VOI pastors give special attention to those men and women who are teachable, available and willing to make personal sacrifices for the good of others, to catch the vision of the church and to become infused with the cultural ethos of the movement.

In addition to on-the-job training under the careful scrutiny of the local pastor, the would-be leader meets regularly for one-on-one times of prayer and accountability with their local pastor, where they are challenged to bring every area of their lives, including their marriage, family and finances, under the lordship of Christ. At each stage appropriate books and other materials are assigned by the pastor, who often reads and analyzes these materials together with aspiring apprentices, making practical applications along the way.

Married couples also meet regularly for mentoring by the local pastor and his wife. Women, especially those married to men who feel called by God to pioneer a new church plant, are also afforded opportunities to develop skills that will be needed to "copastor" a church. A fellowship-wide network exists to disciple and support women within each fellowship, especially those who copastor churches alongside their husbands. At PCCF, women are encouraged to participate in local and regional gatherings called "The Ruth Factor." VOI encourages its women to participate in "United Women in Ministry," which embraces the task of evangelizing and discipling the hurting people of the world with the message of hope and plan of Jesus Christ. "This call involves a commitment to train, develop, inspire and instill within women the desire to fulfill their potential in life with a sense of dignity, belonging and destiny."[22]

Another component in the leadership development paradigms of these two movements is the more formal training offered by the local pastor to those men and women who express a commitment to serve

---

[22]See the official VOI website at <http://www.victoryoutreach.org/ministries/victory-outreach-women.asp>.

and lead locally, or a sense of calling to pioneer a new church. These classes usually meet one night a week for two to three hours and focus on the "core values" and the "foundational beliefs" of their respective movements. In the case of PCCF these values include hearing and responding to the call of God, tapping into the power of the Holy Spirit, radical evangelism, radical discipleship, the importance and role of the local church, the importance of fellowship and accountability, and local and world mission. At PCCF, Pastor Mike Neville established a cherished tradition of reserving one night a week for what is known throughout the movement as "Men's Discipleship." PCCF also started a Bible Training Center at the mother church in Huntington Park. It offers a three-year non-accredited associate degree.[23]

At VOI Sonny Arguinzoni set a similar precedent with weekly gatherings of the "Mighty Men of Valor"—local VO pastors and their "armor bearers," including assistant pastors, rehabilitation home directors, ministry coordinators and small group leaders. Required reading for many of those who participate in these weekly meetings includes *Semper Fidelis: The Character of a Leader*, a book on character building and leadership development by VOI pastor and elder Saul Garcia.[24] At these and other local church and regional functions men gather together for a time of prayer, worship and a special time in the Word of God with their pastors and movement leaders. It is also a time when unity in Christ, camaraderie and a sense of purpose is established and reinforced among the men of Victory Outreach.[25]

In response to the need for more formal training for pastors, church planters and evangelists, Victory Education and Training Institute (VETI) was started in 1984 to provide even more in-depth biblical, spiritual and theological training. Formally known as "Victory Outreach School of Ministry," VETI has also joined hands with Latin American Bible Institute and Azusa Pacific University to provide ad-

---

[23]Donna Neville, interviews with author, March 22, 2007, and November 22, 2009; Larry Neville, interview with author, April 5, 2007.

[24]Saul Garcia, *Semper Fidelis: The Character of a Leader* (San Dimas, Calif.: Vision Multimedia, 2005).

[25]See the official VOI website at <www.victoryoutreach.org/ministries/victory-outreach-men.asp>.

ditional training and accredited degrees for qualified candidates who are already involved in full-time ministry.[26]

More recently, a growing number of single young men and women have asked for formal training to better equip them to assist their local churches and movements. In response, VOI launched Urban Training Centers (UTC). Currently, UTC operates in two locations in the United States: Bridgeport, Connecticut, and Los Angeles, California. Each UTC offers committed young adults an intense six-month or one-year program, where they are immersed in Bible study, personal development and hands-on ministry training under the guidance of successful and mature local VO pastors and their wives.[27]

Others, including Pastor Wilfredo De Jesús at New Life Covenant Church in Chicago (NLCC), operate programs similar to the UTC at Victory Outreach. In 1997 NLCC began Chicago Master's Commission (CMC) in response to the desire of growing numbers of young adults for mentoring and hands-on ministry experience in preparation for future ministry opportunities. CMC offers single young adults an opportunity to live and minister together in the inner city of Chicago, where they are provided with training and diverse ministry opportunities in the context of NLCC.[28] According to Pastor David Marrero, after successful completion of the nine-month program outstanding graduates are invited to work on the staff at CMC for one or two years, where they gain additional ministry and leadership skills that help them to later assume responsibilities as ministry leaders at NLCC. Several full-time staff members at CMC have gone on to become full-time staff and pastors at the church.[29] Pastor Wilfredo De Jesús encourages his young and growing staff to continue their formal theological training at nearby schools like Moody Bible Institute and Wheaton College. But like the leaders of VOI and PCCF, Pastor De Jesús insists that the most important training his pastoral staff receives is in the context of the local congregation, where they are infused with the church's vision,

---

[26]Learn more about VETI at <www.victoryoutreach.org/education/victory-outreach-veti.asp>.
[27]Learn more about UTC at <www.victoryoutreach.org/education/victory-outreach-utc.asp>.
[28]Learn more about CMC at <www.chicagomc.org/>.
[29]David Marrero, interview with author, May 23, 2007.

values and cultural ethos, what he refers to as the DNA of New Life Covenant Church.[30]

THE LOCAL PASTOR AS ORGANIC SEMINARY PROFESSOR

Like the church in Antioch described in the book of Acts, Victory Outreach and Praise Chapel reach those overlooked by the traditional church (Acts 11:19-21). Like the church in Antioch, future evangelists, pioneer church planters and pastors are trained and must demonstrate their evangelistic and leadership skills locally before they are ever sent to plant a new church (Acts 11:25-26; 13:1-3). Every evangelist, pioneer church planter and pastor is taught to be a committed disciple, then trained and mentored locally by caring and dedicated pastors who are modeling daily the life and vocation they too feel called to embrace. Leaders at VOI and PCCF say that on average it takes between five and seven years from the time a man is saved to the point where he is "launched out" to pioneer a new church.[31]

When asked how these movements are able to plant churches that plant more churches in a relatively short period of time, two native-born Hispanic pastors with PCCF agreed that key factors include the experiences gained at the local church and the intimate relationship developed with their local pastor. Pastor Omar Lopez and Pastor Woody Calvary each spoke of the opportunities to serve and lead that were afforded them by Mike Neville. They also spoke of his sincere love for his church, especially for those men and their wives called to pastor new and existing churches. They gratefully recalled that Pastor Mike looked for every opportunity to help them develop their skills to pray publicly, preach powerfully and lead dynamic worship. Omar Lopez added, "[Pastor Mike] loved you and treated you like a friend. . . . Every one of the men our pastor trained and launched would say that Pastor Mike was his best friend."[32]

---

[30]Wilfredo De Jesús, interview with author, May 23, 2007.

[31]Sonny Arguinzoni, interview with author, May 10, 2007; Donna Neville, interviews with author, March 22, 2007, and November 7, 2007; Larry Neville, interview with author, April 5, 2007.

[32]Omar Lopez, interview with author, March 30, 2007; Woody Calvary, interview with author, April 5, 2007.

Victory Outreach and Praise Chapel pastors consistently, reverently and affectionately refer to the pastor of the local church where they were saved and trained as "my pastor." Each of my informants added that the care and mentoring they receive from their pastors doesn't stop when they are "launched out" to pioneer a new church. Again, like the apostle Paul in his relationship with the church in Antioch (Acts 14:26-28), pioneer church planters are regularly invited back to the church from which they were launched out to report on the progress being made, to motivate up-and-coming leaders and to seek advice and receive additional instruction from their pastors. This dynamic relationship between mother and daughter church and pastor and church planter is clearly indispensable to the success of each movement. It is what Pastor Larry Neville at PCCF refers to as "connectivity."[33]

The indispensable role of the local pastor in identifying, recruiting, training and nurturing local ministry leaders, pioneer church planters and pastors is reiterated by virtually all of the pastors consulted for this study. For example, Marc Rivera, senior pastor at Primitive Christian Church on the Lower East Side of Manhattan, insists that intentional and strategic leadership development is vitally important to his ministry and the life of his congregation. Pastor Rivera follows what he refers to as "the sage's model" that he has observed among the Orthodox Jewish leaders in his community. Like those models observed at VOI and PCCF, the sage's model also requires "a strong covenant relationship that lasts a life time."[34] As a modern Christian sage, Pastor Rivera chooses his covenant partners (i.e., his mentees) very carefully.

Selection of potential pastoral candidates follows the "recommended process" outlined earlier by Manuel Ortiz.[35] Pastor Marc Rivera first identifies "faithful members" who demonstrate their commitment to Christ and his church by active and regular participation in the life of the church. Over the years Pastor Rivera has also found that those who tithe and regularly attend early morning prayer meetings consistently

---

[33]Larry Neville, *Connectivity: The Power to Touch the World* (Rancho Cucamonga, Calif.: Planters and Pioneers Publications, 2006).

[34]Marc Rivera, personal correspondence with author, December 5, 2009.

[35]See Ortiz, *Hispanic Challenge*, pp. 143-44.

turn out to be some of the most teachable and trustworthy when later given gender- and age-appropriate responsibilities in the church. In the process of teaching, leading small groups, working with youth, leading worship or coordinating ongoing ministries, future ministry and pastoral candidates distinguish themselves as servant leaders like the household of Stephanas described in 1 Corinthians 16.[36] These are men and women "who have devoted themselves to the service of the saints." They "work and toil" well with others, often doing much more than their share and in the process they "refresh the spirits" of their coworkers in the congregation (1 Cor 16:15-18).

When invited to join an early morning study group, promising servant leaders at Primitive Christian Church jump at the opportunity to learn from and with their pastor, who often invites them to observe and partner with him as he serves the church and community. But Pastor Rivera is quick to say that the privilege of one-on-one time with the pastor brings with it the responsibility of using the knowledge gained from mentoring sessions to more effectively serve the local church and the community. Further one-on-one and small group instruction takes place as questions naturally arise from hands-on involvement in local ministry. Eventually, the leadership potential of these men and women is validated by the members of the congregation who affirm their giftedness and calling for even greater ministry responsibilities. Pastor Mark Rivera also urges qualified leaders to pursue more formal theological training beyond the context of the local church. Some of his apprentices have completed theological degrees at Hartford Seminary and Gordon-Conwell Theological Seminary. The process outlined above mirrors those observed at VOI and PCCF and has supplied Primitive Christian Church with virtually all of its pastoral staff and church planters.

This process resembles the intimate relationship between Paul and Timothy[37] and Jesus and his disciples, especially as the latter is outlined in *The Master Plan of Evangelism*, where Robert Coleman identifies the

---

[36]Marc Rivera, interviews with author, May 19, 2008, April 3, 2009, and December 8, 2009.

[37]See Acts 16:1-3; Phil 2:19-24; and 2 Tim 2:1-2 for NT descriptions of the relationship between Paul and Timothy.

so-called method of leadership development employed by Jesus with his disciples. Steps identified by Coleman include Selection, Association, Consecration, Impartation, Demonstration, Delegation, Supervision and Reproduction.[38] These steps are also readily observed in the approaches of several pastors consulted for this study. This suggests that the leadership development process outlined by Manuel Ortiz in 1993 continues to dominate Hispanic churches, especially those successfully targeting U.S.-born English-dominant Latinos.

CONCLUSION

In his book *LeadershipNext: Changing Leaders in a Changing Culture*, Eddie Gibbs lists several challenges facing church leaders in a postmodern, neo-pagan culture. Each is germane to the Hispanic urban context in the United States. He insists that Christian leaders must respond to each if they are to move their churches beyond the "maintenance model." Victory Outreach, Praise Chapel and Primitive Christian Church in Manhattan have provided concrete examples of many of the proposals for missional leadership presented by Gibbs. First, Gibbs suggests that twenty-first-century church leaders must move "beyond the inherited institution" and lead "mission-focused" communities of disciples.[39] Of necessity, each of the church-planting movements described in this study were forced to create new communities with a missional vision.

Additionally, Gibbs challenges leaders to move "beyond the controlling hierarchy" toward "leading empowered networks of Christ followers."[40] Each of the movements highlighted here resists what Gibbs refers to as the "culture of control."[41] Instead, young leaders are gradually but strategically "empowered" to launch out and start home Bible studies, local ministries and later new church plants. While church planters associated with VOI and PCCF benefit from only short-term

---

[38]Robert Coleman, *The Master Plan of Evangelism* (Old Tappan, N.J.: Fleming H. Revell, 1963).

[39]Eddie Gibbs, *LeadershipNext: Changing Leaders in a Changing Culture* (Downers Grove, Ill.: InterVarsity Press, 2005), p. 38.

[40]Ibid., p. 43.

[41]Ibid., p. 13.

financial assistance, they enjoy ongoing guidance and mentoring by their pastors and work collaboratively with the mother church, which continues to support and encourage their efforts in a dynamic and mutually beneficial relationship.

Eddie Gibbs also recognizes the urgent need to move "beyond the weekly gathering toward building teams engaged in ongoing mission." While weekly gatherings at VOI and PCCF are clearly times of exuberant, charismatic and dynamic worship and fellowship, they also serve to remind the faith community of their vision and purpose "to provide ongoing discipleship training and spiritual guidance for continued development and fruitfulness" leading to the reproduction and multiplication of churches. This naturally leads to the final two recommendations offered by Gibbs. Leaders must move "beyond the gospel of personal self-realization toward service-oriented faith communities."[42] At VOI and PCCF the importance of personal spiritual formation does not drown out the cries and needs of the larger community surrounding the church. By example, pastors demonstrate that the confession "Jesus Christ is Lord" has social implications that require the local church to invest its human, financial and spiritual resources in the neighborhood. Therefore it is quite common to find VOI and PCCF churches running drug rehabilitation homes, gang-prevention programs and after school programs as well as women's shelters in at-risk Hispanic neighborhoods.

Finally, Gibbs challenges leaders to move "beyond the inward focused church toward a society-transforming community."[43] Proudly displayed at VOI and PCCF churches and on official websites are letters of endorsement, recognition and appreciation from local business owners, school boards, police chiefs and municipal, state and federal officials. The latter include letters of recognition from former U.S. Presidents Bill Clinton and George W. Bush. These documents consistently acknowledge each movement for making their respective communities safer and better. Yet few modern day church-planting move-

---

[42]Ibid., pp. 43-44.
[43]Ibid., p. 45.

ments have been so consistently Christ-centered and missional.[44]

Remarkably, leaders at Victory Outreach and Praise Chapel have now been able to pass on their unique Christ-centered and mission-centered vision to a second and even third generation of urban church planters. Perhaps the secret to their success and the success of others is that they have exchanged Saul's armor, that is, the traditional path to pastoral leadership that requires formal theological training, for a familiar sling and a few smooth stones gathered in the context of the local church and at the feet of a visionary pastor.

---

[44]See the official VOI website at <www.victoryoutreach.org/aboutus/victory-outreach-En dorsements.asp>.

THE NEW HISPANIC CHALLENGE

As many of you as were baptized into Christ have
clothed yourselves with Christ. There is no longer Jew or Greek,
there is no longer slave or free, there is no longer male and female;
for all of you are one in Christ Jesus. And if you belong to Christ,
then you are Abraham's offspring, heirs according to the promise.

GALATIANS 3:27-29

IT HAS BEEN ALMOST TWENTY YEARS since the publication of *The His-panic Challenge* by Manuel Ortiz. Thankfully, the ground-breaking study continues to generate much discussion and healthy debate among Latino evangelicals in the United States.[1] However, demographically much has changed since 1993. The Hispanic population has more than doubled, growing from 22 million in 1990 to more than 50 million in 2010.[2] More significantly, unlike the 1980s when immigration ac-counted for most of the growth in the Hispanic population, in the early twenty-first century native births are outpacing immigration as "the key source of growth."[3] Thus we are witnessing a momentous change in the makeup of the Hispanic population in the United States. Today the majority of Hispanics are native born, that is, they are the children and grandchildren of immigrants.[4] Predictably, native-born Latinos are

---

[1]Manuel Ortiz, *The Hispanic Challenge: Opportunities Confronting the Church* (Downers Grove, Ill.: InterVarsity Press, 1993).

[2]See the U.S. Census Bureau, 1970, 1980, 1990, 2000 and 2010 Decennial Censuses.

[3]Richard Fry, "Latino Settlement in the New Century" (Washington, D.C.: Pew Hispanic Center, October 2008), p. i.

[4]Richard Fry and Jeffrey S. Passel, "Latino Children: A Majority Are U.S.-Born Offspring of

overwhelmingly English dominant.[5] Those who are paying special attention to these dramatic changes within the Hispanic community will agree with Juan Francisco Martínez, who acknowledges that "The Latino experience in the United States presents a series of social and cultural complexities that complicate any pastoral ministry effort."[6]

Reflecting on these momentous changes, Professor Martínez remarks, "The Latino community in the United States is dynamic and changing. Every ministry within this community ought to be as well."[7] These demographic and linguistic changes are forcing many Hispanic church leaders to reexamine ministry paradigms designed with foreign-born Spanish-speaking Latinos in mind. After interviewing dozens of Hispanic pastors across the country, I concur with Martínez: "Effective leaders in the Latino community will reorient their ministries to respond to these changes."[8] In this chapter I will identify several significant challenges facing the Hispanic church in the early twenty-first century.

THINKING THEOLOGICALLY ABOUT THE MOMENT OF TRANSITION

In response to this moment of transition in Hispanic communities across the United States, one of the most important tasks facing church leaders is theological. From an evangelical perspective, which views the Bible as the sole authority in matters of faith and practice,[9] that task is best framed as a question: Does the New Testament depict situations faced by the early church that are analogous to those faced by Hispanic churches in the early twenty-first century? If it does, how do the Scriptures inform our response to these new circumstances?

In the passage above from the letter to the Galatians, the apostle

---

Immigrants" (Washington, D.C.: Pew Hispanic Center, May 2008), pp. i, 3.

[5]Pew Hispanic Center and Kaiser Family Foundation, "2002 National Survey of Latinos" (Washington, D.C.: Pew Hispanic Center, December 2002), p. 45.

[6]Juan Francisco Martínez, *Walk with the People: Latino Ministry in the United States* (Nashville: Abingdon, 2008), p. 33.

[7]Juan Francisco Martínez, "Acculturation and the Latino Protestant Church in the United States," in *Los Evangélicos: Portraits of Latino Protestantism in the United States*, ed. Juan F. Martínez and Lindy Scott (Eugene, Ore.: Wipf and Stock, 2009), p. 111.

[8]Martínez, *Walk with the People*, p. 10.

[9]John Bowker, ed., *The Oxford Dictionary of World Religions* (New York: Oxford University Press, 1997), p. 326.

Paul draws attention to *the* moment of transition in the scheme of redemption that finds its fulfillment in the life, death, burial and resurrection of Jesus Christ. The Lord's promise to make of Abraham "a great nation" (Gen 12:3) and in him to bless all the families of the earth has finally become a reality. Now in Christ Jesus we "are all children of God through faith" (Gal 3:26). This also means that anyone (e.g., Jew, Greek, slave, free, male or female) who had been baptized into Christ and thereby been clothed with Christ was also an offspring, or descendent, of Abraham.[10]

The practical consequences of this moment of transition were not overlooked by the Jewish Christians, especially those in the Diaspora, who were watching the numbers of uncircumcised Gentiles swell within the ranks of the early church. An important question arose, which prompted the convening of the Jerusalem council described in Acts 15: As far as the Gentiles were concerned, what were to be the minimum requirements for salvation and full acceptance within the church? Some insisted, "It is necessary for them to be circumcised and ordered to keep the law of Moses" (Acts 15:5). In other words, they demanded that the Gentiles "acculturate" and then "assimilate" into the dominant group (i.e., observant Jews). Fortunately, the apostles and the elders in Jerusalem rejected this proposal and instead responded with the following words found in Acts 15:28-29: "For it has seemed good to the Holy Spirit and to us to impose on you [Gentiles] no further burden than these essentials: that you abstain from what has been sacrificed to idols and from blood and from what is strangled and from fornication. If you keep yourselves from these, you will do well."

The remainder of Paul's ministry as it is described in Acts and in several New Testament epistles includes an ongoing battle with what I call the "Jewish mono-culturalists," that is, the circumcision group, who refused to yield to the will of the Holy Spirit and the apostles.[11] Even after the Jerusalem council they continued to insist that if Gentile Chris-

---

[10]See Everett Ferguson, *Baptism in the Early Church: History, Theology, and Liturgy in the First Five Centuries* (Grand Rapids: Eerdmans, 2009) for an excellent study of the nature and purpose of baptism in the teaching and ministry of the apostle Paul.

[11]See Acts 11:1-18; 15:1-5; Gal 2:11-18; 5:2-4; and Phil 3:2-3.

tians desired to be saved they needed to fully adopt the ways of the Jewish Christians, including circumcision, the Mosaic dietary laws and sabbath observances. Biblical scholars contend that the unwillingness of the circumcision group to recognize the "moment of transition" inaugurated by the death, burial and resurrection of Christ helped to precipitate the "irrevocable split of church and synagogue." The cross marked "the end of the old age and the beginning of God's new creation."[12]

In *Santa Biblia: Reading the Bible Through Hispanic Eyes*, Justo González reflects on the continued reluctance of the early church to embrace the growing number of Gentiles. He observes that from the moment the early church heard about the conversion of Cornelius (Acts 11:1-18), Jewish Christians, including the apostles, manifested symptoms of what he calls the "Jonah syndrome." That is, they desired to grow through crosscultural outreach, but without a corresponding willingness to embrace the process of *mestizaje* that would inevitably result in changes in the church reflecting the dynamic mixture of both cultures. Not only did the early church struggle with the Jonah syndrome, but González maintains that many contemporary churches suffer from this problem as well.

> Likewise, there are many in our old-line denominations who are constantly calling for more evangelistic effort, but who balk at the changes this would bring about in the church. They want the church to grow in numbers, but not to change in composition. They want to evangelize, but they seem to think that the gospel is only for people like them—of their own race, class, culture, and education level.[13]

This observation can also be made of Hispanic evangelical churches that desire to grow in numbers but not at the expense of their ethnic identity, cultural and religious ethos or their language of preference. Many churches dominated by Spanish-dominant immigrants want to grow, and in many cases are growing at phenomenal rates.[14] Some stra-

---

[12]Richard B. Hays, "The Letter of Paul to the Galatians," in *The Harper Collins Study Bible*, rev. ed., ed. Wayne A. Meeks (New York: HarperCollins, 2006), p. 1973.

[13]Justo L. González, *Santa Biblia: Reading the Bible Through Hispanic Eyes* (Nashville: Abingdon, 1996), p. 54.

[14]For example, in 2007 *Outreach Magazine* highlighted *Iglesia Cristiana Segadores de Vida*, the church copastored by Ruddy and Maria Gracia in Hollywood, Florida, as the fastest growing

tegically target the generation of their children and grandchildren. But their reluctance to accommodate the cultural and linguistic needs and cultural preferences of native-born Latinos inhibits their success. Jose Garcia, State Supervisor of Latino Churches in California, Church of God of the Prophecy states it even more emphatically: "The church that resists accepting the usage of English in its different ministries is destined to lose a generation, particularly when children, who in spite of following many of our customs and traditions, communicate better in English."[15]

In his efforts to address the growing tensions between Jewish and Gentile believers in the early church, the apostle Paul reminds readers that in Christ God is creating a brand new humanity or race: "For [Jesus Christ] is our peace; in his flesh he has made both groups into one and has broken down the dividing wall, that is, the hostility between us" (Eph 2:14). Clearly this new race is a *mestizo* (mixed) people, indicated by his statement that God "has made both groups into one." However, *mestizaje* implies change, and like the early church depicted in Acts, most churches resist change. Justo González acknowledges that "a certain instinct tells us that radical evangelism, in our society would bring about the conversion, not only of unbelievers, but also of the church. For many, that would be too threatening. Therefore we make certain that mission flows only in one direction: that the center can affect the periphery, but not vice versa."[16]

In the same way, this study has drawn attention to the dramatic changes in the history and development of Hispanic evangelical ministries in the United States. The successful inclusion of growing numbers of U.S.-born English-dominant Latinos in Hispanic evangelical churches challenges denominational leaders and local pastors to reexamine many of their traditional ministry paradigms, especially the assumption that Hispanic ministry is synonymous with Spanish-language ministry.

---

church in the U.S. See Ed Stetzer, "The 2007 Outreach 100, America's Largest and Fastest-Growing Churches," *Outreach Magazine* 6 (Fall 2007), special ed.

[15]Quoted in Martínez, *Walk with the People*, p. 111.

[16]Ibid., p. 55.

Fortunately, the case studies presented in this study reveal that growing numbers of Hispanic evangelical churches recognize the historic moment of transition and are making appropriate adjustments to accommodate the ever-increasing number of English-dominant Latinos, especially children, teens and young adults. The findings presented here parallel those described by Teresa Chávez Sauceda in her study of Hispanic mainline churches. "What Hispanic congregations are recognizing is that if our children are to be the church of the future, they must be the church today. Their participation in the church needs to be meaningful for them both as Christians and as Hispanics in order for them to feel that it is a place where they belong."[17]

Chávez Sauceda insists that Hispanic children and young people who are not fluent in Spanish will be marginalized by Spanish-only worship experiences unless some portion of the worship service is in English. At the same time, she insists that the Hispanic church must also maintain its commitment to provide "worship in Spanish for those older generations and recent immigrants who are most comfortable speaking Spanish." As in the case of churches highlighted in this study, "Hispanic congregations have shown both courage and creativity as they have confronted this issue and explored a variety of ways of responding to the needs of the congregation."[18]

OVERCOMING HISPANIC CULTURAL AND SPIRITUAL SUPERIORITY

Why do many Hispanic church leaders continue to resist the changes that have helped other churches grow significantly without compromising what they understand to be the essential nature of the gospel? Recent studies suggest important social as well as theological reasons for opposing the expanded use of English and more accommodating stances toward native-born Latinos who do not share the linguistic, cultural and religious idiosyncrasies of foreign-born Spanish-dominant members.

Cultural resistance. In his study of Hispanic Protestant churches,

---

[17]Teresa Chávez Sauceda, "Becoming a Mestizo Church," in *¡Alabadle! Hispanic Christian Worship,* ed. Justo L. González (Nashville: Abingdon, 1996), pp. 92-93.
[18]Ibid.

Edwin Hernández noted that sociologically, traditional Spanish-speaking churches help foreign-born Latinos adapt to life in the United States while at the same time serving as "an important mechanism for sustaining cultural values, language, and practices."[19] Consequently, for some churches dominated by foreign-born Latinos, incorporating English-language programs and ministries to accommodate native-born Latinos undermines their efforts to sustain and reinforce the values, language and practices of the immigrant generation.

Reverend Samuel Rodríguez, president of the National Hispanic Christian Leadership Conference (NHCLC), is one of the most well-known and respected Hispanic evangelicals in the United States. In the United States and Puerto Rico the NHCLC serves more than thirty-one thousand Hispanic evangelical congregations in more than seventy-four denominations, with a total membership of over sixteen million members.[20] As president of the NHCLC, Samuel Rodríguez has had a front-row seat and has been extended invitations to preach in hundreds of Hispanic churches in the United States. Given his extensive knowledge of the Hispanic evangelical church in the United States, I asked him what he perceived to be at the heart of the ongoing debate to incorporate more English ministries and programs in Hispanic evangelical churches to accommodate native-born Latinos. He reiterated what several pastors consulted in this study have stated: "Some first-generation pastors and Christians are driven by a desire to preserve their culture. Consequently they are isolationists."[21] Instead, Hispanic church leaders would do well to consider the wisdom expressed by first-generation Latinos like Juan Carlos Ortiz, pastor emeritus of the Hispanic Department at the Crystal Cathedral in California: "If our effort to maintain our culture in a foreign country makes our children leave the church, we have gained nothing."[22]

---

[19]Edwin I. Hernández, "Moving from the Cathedral to Storefront Churches: Understanding Religious Growth and Decline Among Latino Protestants," in *Protestantes/Protestants: Hispanic Christianity Within Mainline Traditions*, ed. David Maldonado Jr. (Nashville: Abingdon, 1999), p. 223.

[20]Learn more about the National Hispanic Christian Leadership Conference at <www.nhclc .org/>.

[21]Samuel Rodríguez, interview with author, December 10, 2009.

[22]Quoted in Martínez, *Walk with the People*, p. 110.

David Morales, associate pastor at Primitive Christian Church in Manhattan, believes that the issue ultimately comes down to different priorities and philosophies of ministry. "Hispanic pastors need to ask themselves, 'Is our primary responsibility to minister to the same people, people who are already saved, people who have been faithful members of the church for twenty to thirty years, or do we address the needs of the changing neighborhood and those of our young people who are hungry for the Lord but often cannot relate to our message or style?'" Reflecting on his earlier years growing up attending a traditional Spanish-speaking church in New York, Morales recalls,

> Our pastor, a dedicated servant of God was born and raised in Puerto Rico, where he also received his [ministerial] training. As a teenager attending our Spanish church, my friends and I couldn't relate to the pastor's stories about life in Puerto Rico. We had never cut sugar cane! We had been born and raised in New York. What we were looking for was a Hispanic ministry that was able to challenge us intellectually and speak to where we were. That is what ultimately led me to *Primitiva*.[23]

In contrast, David Marrero recalls watching his senior pastor, Wilfredo De Jesús, cast a vision for a new ministry paradigm that would help *Iglesia Cristiana Palestina* become more responsive to the diverse community of Humboldt Park. David recalls the apprehension of many older members of the 125-member Spanish-speaking Pentecostal church when Pastor Wilfredo De Jesús began proposing far-reaching changes at *Palestina*. "Many of the older members were afraid of what might happen." They were afraid of what the other pastors and churches in the area would say about them if they gave up some of their traditional practices and relaxed some of the manmade restrictions that defined them as *evangélicos*. Others were afraid that members who disapproved of the changes would leave. But Marrero recalls the resolve and courage of Pastor De Jesús who was willing and ready to do whatever it would take to reach the city for Christ, including offering English services and changing the name from *Iglesia Cristiana Palestina* to New

---

[23]David Morales, interview with author, May 20, 2008.

Life Covenant Church. Explosive growth soon followed. "At the end of the day we had seen the hand of God move among us. Then everyone got on board."[24]

My informants have consistently argued that what is desperately needed are more first-generation pastors like Aureliano Flores, pastor emeritus at Church of the Redeemer in Baldwin Park, California. Our churches need men and women who hear the Lord remind them, "I didn't call you to preach the gospel in English or Spanish. I called you to preach the gospel!"[25] We need men and women more dedicated to making disciples of all the nations than they are to preserving the language, culture and religious traditions of their countries of origin. To echo the apostle Paul in Galatians 3:28, we need to recall that *"there is no longer* foreign-born or native-born Latino . . . *for all of* us *are one in Christ Jesus."*

Theological resistance. In addition to the commitment to preserve the culture and traditions of the immigrant generation, there are also theological presuppositions that strengthen the resolve to resist the call to accommodate the linguistic and cultural preferences of native-born English-dominant Latinos. For instance, Christians are called to be holy in all their conduct (1 Pet 1:14-16) which above all else is characterized by "nonconformity" to the pattern of this world (Rom 12:2). To the first generation, their cherished traditions and prohibitions are not viewed as "cultural preferences," but rather as reflecting the value of personal and communal holiness *(la santidad)*, "without which no one will see the Lord" (Heb 12:14). Therefore, for many first-generation Latino Christians it is untenable to consider accommodating the younger generation's needs and preferences, many of which have been influenced by the world. Samuel Solivan-Román sheds additional light on this theological source of resistance. He argues that many Hispanic evangelicals "understand themselves to be the bulwark against death and the forces of evil that are overwhelming the world. They are a fortress against the cultural forces that seek to destroy them and their value system—a system that they understand as reflecting the values of

---

[24]David Marrero, interview with author, May 23, 2008.
[25]Aureliano Flores, interview with author, June 6, 2007.

the kingdom of God and their Lord Jesus Christ."[26]

While many native-born Hispanic Christians understand and respect the theological assumptions and commitments of *los ancianos* (the
older members of the congregation), to many some of the traditions and
corresponding prohibitions appear legalistic and nonsensical. One of
my informants who wished to remain anonymous is a twenty-five-year-
old pastor's son, a devoted Christian and a gifted musician who leads
dynamic worship in his father's thriving storefront Spanish-speaking
Pentecostal church. Over the years he has watched many of his peers,
frustrated with what they perceive as "blind legalism," leave the church
when they become teenagers or when they go off to college. A few others have chosen to join more "progressive churches" considered liberal
by the older generation. He said that many teenage boys and young
men saw no logical connection between their preference for long hair
(or shaved heads), earrings or baggy pants and the "worldliness" that
the pastor and older members feared would creep into the church.
Likewise young women saw no reasonable correlation between their
preference for using modest amounts of makeup and wearing pants to
church and the lack of holiness these symbolized to the first generation. Frustrated, many young men and women have left the church.

Youth Pastor David Marrero, a second-generation Puerto Rican,
sees the same phenomena among many teens who come from traditional Spanish-speaking churches to participate in the youth program
at New Life Covenant Church in Chicago. They come from churches
where, from the perspective of the teens and young adults, "tradition
and the preferences of the older members take precedence over reaching
the lost, especially the youth."[27]

Egypt or the Promised Land? In all fairness to the immigrant generation, frustrated native-born Hispanic Christians are often unable or
unwilling to see their own "subculture" and the broader American society through the eyes of foreign-born Hispanic Christians. For example, many Spanish-dominant Latinos do not equate the United States

---

[26]Samuel Solivan-Román, "Hispanic Pentecostal Worship," in *¡Alabadle! Hispanic Christian
Worship*, ed. Justo L. González (Nashville: Abingdon, 1996), p. 45.
[27]David Marrero, interview with author, May 23, 2008.

with the Promised Land or the "Chosen Nation" as do many American Christians, including many U.S.-born Latinos.[28] Instead, many foreign-born Latinos draw analogies between their experience in the United States and that of the Hebrews in Egypt. Like the sons of Jacob (Gen 46–50), many Hispanic immigrants leave their beloved homelands and come to United States (i.e., Egypt) for one primary reason: to survive. They come to the United States because here they can carry on until they are in a position to return to their *patria* (homeland) to live out their dreams. In the meantime they resolve like the descendents of Jacob to maintain a necessary distance from the Egyptians (i.e., Anglo Americans) and their materialistic and decadent culture, pejoratively referred to as *"el mundo"* ("the world").

Consequently Latino evangelicals, especially the foreign born, feel compelled to create spiritual as well as cultural ghettos like the land of Goshen (Gen 46:28) where they can sustain and reinforce the culture, values, language and practices of their *patria* while they "live in exile" surrounded by a foreign, hostile and worldly society. Seen sympathetically from this standpoint, incorporating English and accommodating the cultural preferences of highly assimilated Latinos is tantamount to opening the doors of the church to "the forces of evil that are overwhelming the world."[29] Dr. Isaac Canales, pastor of Mission Ebenezer Family Church in Carson, California, reminds us that many well-meaning and pious first-generation Latino Christians sincerely believe they must resist assimilation and acculturation, including encouraging the use of English in the church, because *"el diablo habla ingles"* ("the devil speaks English").[30]

The devil is bilingual. But several pastors introduced in this study insist that statements like *"el diablo habla ingles"* and regular references to the decadent culture of *los anglos* (i.e., the dominant group) reveal a

---

[28]See Richard T. Hughes, *Myths America Lives By* (Urbana: University of Illinois Press, 2004). Hughes examines the sources of such American myths as the Chosen Nation, Nature's Nation, the Christian Nation, the Millennial Nation and the Innocent Nation. He then offers a critique of each myth from the perspective of those marginalized by the dominant group (e.g., African Americans and Native Americans).

[29]Solivan-Román, "Hispanic Pentecostal Worship," p. 45.

[30]Isaac Canales, interview with author, March 15, 2007.

sense of cultural superiority prevalent among many first-generation Hispanic evangelicals. Wilfredo De Jesús, pastor of New Life Covenant Church in Chicago, has heard many well-meaning Hispanic church leaders repeatedly remark that *"el español es el idioma del cielo"* ("Spanish is the language spoken in heaven"). Pastor De Jesús insists that statements like these betray "a racist and ethnocentric attitude" that unnecessarily alienates and offends English-dominant native-born Latinos.[31] Manuel Ortiz also noted that the Latino ethnocentrism described by these pastors brings with it an anti-American bias that inadvertently reinforces "the paradox of living in two hostile worlds." As a result, young U.S.-born Latinos are unintentionally excluded from the church in favor of the foreign-born and second-generation Latinos who embrace "the value system of their native country—rural, monolingual, embodying conservative Hispanic values."[32] In response to the unconscious cultural superiority revealed in such statements as *"el diablo habla ingles"* and *"el español es el idioma del cielo,"* Dr. Isaac Canales reminds members who long for the good old days when the church was entirely Spanish speaking that *el diablo es bilingüe* (the devil is bilingual)![33]

Many pastors introduced in this study have also been obliged to address Spanish-speaking members' prejudices against native-born English-speaking Latinos. Many native-born English-speaking Latinos would agree with Teresa Chávez Sauceda, who reminds us that "while language is a major carrier of culture, it is not the only one."[34] Sadly, however, many young Latinos like *Nuyorican* Orlando Crespo continue to feel discriminated against by first-generation *Boricua* based on their inability to speak Spanish well or at all. "Spanish-dominant Latinos will still judge me based on how well I speak [Spanish], based on an unwritten rule that to be Latino you must speak Spanish well."[35]

Mike Castillo, young adult pastor at *Iglesia Alpha & Omega* in Miami, shares similar sentiments. "I learned to read the Bible in English, after

---

[31]Wilfredo De Jesús, interview with author, May 23, 2008.
[32]Ortiz, *The Hispanic Challenge*, p. 63.
[33]Canales, interview.
[34]Chávez Sauceda, "Becoming a Mestizo Church," p. 94.
[35]Orlando Crespo, *Being Latino in Christ: Finding Wholeness in Your Ethnic Identity* (Downers Grove, Ill.: InterVarsity Press, 2003), p. 36.

I was saved. Today, I still can't preach in Spanish." But then again neither can many of the hundreds of Cuban-American young adults in his ministry. Nonetheless, he insists that "we are still Latino. Being Cuban is in our blood, even if we don't speak Spanish." Castillo's comments validate the observation made by Pulitzer Prize-winning journalist Héctor Tobar, a second-generation Guatemalan who has mapped out the complex national identity of U.S.-born Latinos like himself. "We embrace our *latinidad* with more fervor even as our mestizo roots in a distant homeland become more distant."[36] This is evident among native-born Latinos like Pastor Mike Castillo, who in spite of not speaking Spanish well or at all are drawn to what they perceive as *lo cubano* (that which is Cuban), *lo dominicano, lo mexicano, lo puertorriqueño* and so on. Like many other second- and third-generation Latinos in South Florida, Pastor Mike Castillo looks forward to the day when the older generation is not ashamed of him and his peers for not speaking Spanish, or for speaking it poorly.[37]

Similarly, many native-born Latinos discriminate against first-generation Hispanics based on their inability to speak English well or at all and for being uninformed about important cultural idiosyncrasies of the dominant group. Once again, the words of Manuel Ortiz continue to be relevant: "Linguistic realities should never be used to exclude, remove or alienate others, especially those of similar cultural roots. Only when we begin to accept others, listen and learn from them with great interest, and allow ourselves to enter into each other's world will we be able to reverse the language limitations of the second and third generations."[38]

MORE THAN ENGLISH SERVICES AND PROGRAMS

We have also observed that many Hispanic church leaders understand that the needs of native-born English-dominant Latinos go beyond a preference for programs and ministries in English. More challenging is the need to recognize that the barrier between foreign-born Latinos

---

[36]Héctor Tobar, *Translation Nation: Defining a New American Identity in the Spanish-Speaking United States* (New York: Riverhead Books, 2005), p. 304.
[37]Mike Castillo, interview with author, June 30, 2008.
[38]Ortiz, *Hispanic Challenge*, p. 87.

and U.S.-born Latinos is not just linguistic but also cultural.

Contextualized worship. One place where this is most obvious is in corporate worship, where linguistic and cultural differences between foreign-born and native-born Latinos often require significant adjustments in styles of attire, music, worship and preaching. However, as we have seen in this study, even among highly acculturated Latinos Hispanic ethnic identity and loyalty often persist. Therefore responsive pastors and churches are careful to integrate distinctly Latino flavors even in worship services conducted entirely in English. For example, popular styles of music used in English worship services among English-speaking Latinos include salsa, regeton, hip-hop, rap and rock as well as contemporary Christian music in English.

Passionate worship. Careful observers have also noted that across generations, passion is still an important component of Hispanic culture, even among U.S-born Latinos. For example, in Hispanic evangelical worship services adapted to second- and third-generation Latinos, sermons and altar calls are generally much shorter than in worship services tailored to the foreign born. But as Samuel Solivan-Román has observed, they are seldom less passionate. "Most that we do is done with enthusiasm, whether it be socializing, working, or praising God."[39] This is not surprising since among Latino evangelicals the church is regularly embraced as one's extended family, the household or *familia de Dios* (Eph 2:19) "in a way that the dominant culture finds difficult to understand!"[40] This ecclesiology implies that the Hispanic church is the place where as Latinos we naturally and safely express our deepest and most powerful emotions to God and to one another without concerning ourselves with *"¿qué dirán?"* ("What will *they* say?").[41] As one would expect, in churches across the United States that successfully target native-born English-speaking Latinos, corporate worship services are enthusiastic and Spirit-filled family gatherings where joy and

---

[39]Solivan-Román, "Hispanic Pentecostal Worship," p. 55.

[40]González, *Santa Biblia*, p. 109.

[41]"A growing fervor in the expression of worship" has also been observed in Hispanic Baptist churches. See Miguel Angel Darino, "What Is Different About Hispanic Baptist Worship?" in *¡Alabadle! Hispanic Christian Worship*, ed. Justo L. González (Nashville: Abingdon, 1996), p. 88.

sorrow are expressed in uninhibited ways—because language is never a barrier to heartfelt worship.

PREACHING AND MODELING A HOLISTIC GOSPEL IN THE BARRIO

Samuel Rodríguez of the NHCLC has observed that first-generation pastors and Christians are often characteristically "vertically focused," giving their attention primarily if not exclusively to meeting people's spiritual needs, especially the need to be saved and transformed into "counter-cultural" disciples of Jesus Christ. Therefore, verbal proclamation of the gospel dominates the approaches to ministry among many foreign-born pastors and Christians.[42] We have observed that in addition to preaching the gospel, many U.S.-born Latino Christians are also "horizontally focused," concerned with addressing people's felt needs through relief, development and social justice initiatives.

This study has demonstrated that a growing number of multigenerational Hispanic churches and multiethnic predominately Hispanic churches are embracing holistic approaches to ministry which they believe emulate the public ministry of Jesus Christ.[43] Taking their cue from the ministry of Jesus, leaders at these churches agree with Professor Samuel Escobar who observes that "through teaching, preaching and healing, the work of Jesus reached and transformed people in all aspects of their lives, so we can conclude without any doubt that *Jesus' mission was holistic.*"[44]

Nevertheless, many conservative Hispanic evangelicals continue to express serious concerns when Latino church leaders begin talking about "holistic ministry." To some it sounds like advocacy for the so-called social gospel. Others express concern that a holistic approach will divert attention and valuable human and material resources from what really matters, getting people saved! As we observed earlier in this study, juxtaposing evangelism and social responsibility is a false di-

---

[42]Samuel Rodríguez, interview with author, December 10, 2009.

[43]See chapters two and three of this study for detailed descriptions and analyses of the multigenerational churches and multiethnic predominately Hispanic churches highlighted in this study.

[44]Samuel Escobar, *The New Global Mission: The Gospel from Everywhere to Everyone* (Downers Grove, Ill.: InterVarsity Press, 2003), p. 143.

chotomy.[45] The late Orlando Costas stated it more simply, "It is when the gospel makes 'somebody' out of 'nobodies' of society, when it restores the self-worth of the marginalized, when it enables the oppressed to have a reason for hope, when it empowers the poor to struggle and suffer for liberation and peace, that it is truly good news of a new order of life—the saving power of God (Rom 1:16)."[46]

This is exactly what I heard from pastors like Marc Rivera at Primitive Christian Church on the Lower East Side of Manhattan. Rivera is now mentoring younger pastors like David Morales, who respond in the following manner to those who question his ministry priorities: "At Primitive Christian Church we are concerned that you are saved; but we are also going to speak up when we see injustice, and seek the peace of the city. It may not sound like what is traditionally associated with the gospel, but it is the gospel. We speak for those who do not have a voice."[47] That is precisely the point: a truly holistic approach to ministry *is* gospel, good news to the vast majority of Latinos who experience residential segregation, employment discrimination, social and economic neglect and political isolation.[48]

Samuel Solivan-Román has observed like many of the pastors introduced in this study that the experience of "living in the belly of the beast, of knowing hunger in the land of good and plenty, of being poor on the streets of gold provides a different perspective and a different set of questions about who God is and what God is doing in the world."[49] One such question is, "What kind of church is needed to respond to the urgent matters faced by crucified people?"[50] Church leaders introduced in this study insist that what is urgently needed in

---

[45]See chapter four for a detailed description and analysis of the holistic approaches to ministry in the churches highlighted in this study.

[46]Orlando E. Costas, "Evangelism from the Periphery: The Universality of Galilee," in *Voces: Voices from the Hispanic Church*, ed. Justo L. González (Nashville: Abingdon, 1992), p. 17.

[47]David Morales, interview with author, May 20, 2008.

[48]Miguel A. De La Torre and Edwin David Aponte, *Introducing Latino/a Theologies* (Maryknoll, N.Y.: Orbis, 2001), p. 54.

[49]Samuel Solivan-Román, "The Need for a North American Hispanic Theology," in *Mestizo Christianity: Theology from the Latino Perspective*, ed. Arturo J. Bañuelas (Maryknoll, N.Y.: Orbis, 1995), p. 45.

[50]Harold J. Recinos, *Who Comes in the Name of the Lord? Jesus at the Margins* (Nashville: Abingdon, 1997), p. 137.

the barrio are more churches that "seek to accompany the poor and outsiders on the journey that alters society for the common good of all creation."[51]

Predictably, we see a growing number of Hispanic evangelical churches offering preventative and educational services in poor, underserved and working-class neighborhoods. These include afterschool programs, charter schools, job skill programs, life skill labs and health clinics. Still others offer parenting and marriage seminars, mentoring programs and even soccer and little leagues. In at-risk urban neighborhoods it is also common to find Hispanic evangelical churches planning, organizing and running modest as well as massive food distribution programs, Christ-centered recovery programs and residential rehabilitation programs for those trapped in the alcohol, drug and gang culture that plagues many barrios where dropout rates and teenage pregnancy rates are among the highest in the nation.

The best of the creative and holistic ministries highlighted in this study reject the false dichotomy between evangelism and social responsibility still advocated by many evangelical churches and denominations. Instead, they are committed to imitate their Savior who is remembered not just for his verbal proclamation of the good news of the kingdom, but also for going "about doing good and healing all who were oppressed by the devil" (Acts 10:38). Their Lord is the same one who sent his disciples "out to proclaim the kingdom of God *and* to heal" (Lk 9:2, emphasis added). In other words, they recognize along with those associated with the Lausanne Movement[52] that:

> To proclaim Jesus as Lord and Savior (evangelism) has social implications, since it summons people to repent of social as well as personal sins, and to live a new life of righteousness and peace in the new society which challenges the old.
>
> To give food to the hungry (social responsibility) has evangelistic

[51]Ibid., p. 136.

[52]I was honored to serve as a U.S. delegate at Cape Town 2010: The Third Lausanne Congress on World Evangelization (October 2010). I was nominated by my peers at the National Hispanic Christian Leadership Conference, where I have served as a board member since 2009.

implications, since good works of love, if done in the name of Christ, are a demonstration and commendation of the gospel.[53]

LEADERSHIP DEVELOPMENT FOR THE MOMENT OF TRANSITION

As my informants can readily testify, sensitively but intentionally moving a Hispanic congregation beyond the immigrant church model toward a multigenerational, multilingual model is a daunting task to say the least. They also agree that assisting churches dominated by the immigrant generation to overcome the cultural and spiritual superiority that inadvertently marginalizes many U.S.-born English-dominant Latinos is a formidable undertaking. These tasks seem overwhelming if not impossible when one adds to this the responsibility and urgency of raising up indigenous leaders committed to holistic approaches to ministry. Unfortunately, many promising Hispanic leaders are not qualified or in a position to take advantage of even the best urban theological education programs like the Center for Urban Ministerial Education (CUME) at Gordon-Conwell Theological Seminary. Instead, they must rely almost exclusively on the training they receive in the local church. Fortunately, experts like Edgar Elliston remind us that in the leadership development process the local church is too often overlooked or devalued:

> Local churches provide the primary arenas for identifying, selecting, and developing the whole range of Christian leaders. A person may attend a Christian college, university or seminary for a training interlude of a few years, but his/her "home" congregation continues to provide the proving ground for continuing development and lifelong service. Hence a focus on church-based or home-grown leadership development is crucial.[54]

By necessity, each of the churches highlighted in this study has rediscovered the crucial and God-given role of the local church in the

---

[53]The International Consultation on the Relationship Between Evangelism and Social Responsibility, Grand Rapids, Michigan, June 19-25, 1982, "Grand Rapids Report on Evangelism and Social Responsibility: An Evangelical Commitment," in *Making Christ Known: Historic Mission Documents From the Lausanne Movement, 1974-1989,* ed. John Stott (Grand Rapids: Eerdmans, 1996), p. 182.

[54]Edgar J. Elliston, *Home Grown Leaders* (Pasadena, Calif.: William Carey Library, 1992), p. 4.

leadership development process. In fact, Manuel Ortiz observes that leadership development in the context of the local church is normative in many if not most Hispanic churches where future leaders are first recognized by their "calling" before they are recognized for their credentials.[55] Similarly, Edwin Hernández has noted that in many cases the promising leader's calling is authenticated by the local pastor and members "who recognize the calling as being legitimate due to the gifts of preaching, teaching, and counseling they exhibit."[56]

Thankfully, the apparent lack of "theological education" or "theological literacy" among many Hispanic church leaders is often more than compensated for by the competencies gained at the level of the local church, where special attention is often given first to character development, spiritual formation and the development of ministry skills critical for those ministering in the Hispanic urban context. However, Pastor Marc Rivera at Primitive Christian Church on the Lower East Side of Manhattan urges us to remember that local leadership development initiatives must be intentional, strategic and relational.[57] Under the careful supervision of the local pastoral staff, ministry skills are first modeled and then practiced, usually in the context of an ongoing small group ministry like that observed at *Vida Abundante* in San Antonio. These skills include the ability to give a sincere yet compelling personal testimony which provides believers as well as prebelievers with "irrefutable evidence that 'Christianity works.'"[58] Usually within the context of a small group, men and women are also taught to pray publically with the passion and conviction that comes from genuine faith and trust in God, knowledge of his will and desire to edify those who are listening. Future leaders also gain the skills necessary to lead Bible studies, preach, lead public worship and provide pastoral care and counseling. Above all, up-and-coming leaders are taught to evangelize and disciple others for active and effective participation in the

---

[55]Ortiz, *The Hispanic Challenge*, pp. 143-44.
[56]Edwin I. Hernández, "The Religious Experience of Latino/a Protestant Youth," in *Pathways of Hope and Faith Among Hispanic Teens*, ed. Ken Johnson-Mondragón (Stockton, Calif.: Instituto Fe y Vida, 2007), p. 308.
[57]Marc Rivera, interviews with author, May 19, 2008, April 3, 2009, and December 8, 2009.
[58]Hernández, "Religious Experience of Latino/a Protestant Youth," p. 310.

ongoing mission of the local church. Those recognized as possessing exceptional giftedness in these areas are usually given greater roles within the congregation, ultimately leading some into full-time ministry positions. When their call is confirmed, the most gifted are sometimes sent to plant new congregations. This was clearly seen in the successful leadership development paradigms at Victory Outreach International and Praise Chapel Christian Fellowship, two church-planting movements that have planted hundreds of congregations in at-risk Hispanic neighborhoods during the past four decades.

Whenever the option is available, pastors highlighted in this study encourage committed members, ministry candidates and pastoral staff to further their education. Local Bible institutes staffed with experienced local, regional and denominational church leaders often provide the first phase of formal theological education. Each provides more in-depth biblical, spiritual and theological training that cannot be obtained through traditional adult education programs or small group Bible studies. But each is tailored to the needs of local church members, many of whom do not meet the minimum requirements for enrollment in formal ministerial training programs.[59] Some Bible colleges and Christian universities will even give credit for such work toward associate and even bachelor's degrees.

The cases studies presented here also remind us that leadership development becomes the critical issue for reaching Hispanic young people. Church leaders must commit themselves to nurture young leaders who reflect the diversity of the community. This means that in Hispanic communities where the fastest growing segment of the population is native born and English dominant, the church's emerging leaders must also be from this group. In foreign mission work this is referred to as the "indigenization of leadership," which is considered indispensible for establishing an indefinitely reproducible mission or ministry paradigm. Ken Johnson-Mondragón urges local leaders to empower promising young leaders "to create activities, programs, and environ-

---

[59]For examples of local training programs see "Victory Education and Training Center" of Victory Outreach International (www.vetionline.com). For options in Miami see the "Bible Institute" at *Iglesia Alpha & Omega* and the "School of Leadership" at *Ministerios Coral Park.*

ments that are culturally appropriate, relevant to the needs of their peers, and in harmony with the gospel."[60] Here again local leadership development programs designed specifically with younger native-born Latinos in mind are producing a generation of servant leaders committed to both the Great Commission and the Great Commandment, that is, to preaching good news and doing good works.[61]

But Hispanic scholars like Alvin Padilla, professor and director for CUME at Gordon-Conwell, and his colleague Eldín Villafañe also remind us that the Hispanic church must also challenge Christian institutions of higher learning, especially seminaries, to rethink what "theological competency" looks like in the Hispanic American context. Too many seminaries assume cultural and theological perspectives that do not reflect the at-risk underserved context of Hispanic churches in the United States in the twenty-first century. In *Seek the Peace of the City: Reflections on Urban Ministry,* Eldín Villafañe describes six essential elements or criteria for evaluating the effectiveness of seminary-based urban theological education programs from a Hispanic urban perspective. These criteria include a clear vision of the program's target constituency, the investment of valuable resources, a holistic curriculum, the blessing of the host community, full integration into the life of the host seminary, and a long-term financial commitment to the program.[62] Nevertheless, the future leadership of the Hispanic church in the United States does not depend on contextually appropriate seminary-based theological education programs. Instead, the apostle Paul reminds us in Ephesians 4:11-13 that servant leaders will emerge from within the local church where they are nurtured by gifted and caring evangelists, pastors and teachers provided by Jesus Christ for the building up of his church.

Readers will detect that the challenges outlined in this chapter arise

---

[60]Ken Johnson-Mondragón, "Socioreligious Demographics of Hispanic Teenagers," in *Pathways of Hope and Faith Among Hispanic Teens,* ed. Ken Johnson-Mondragón (Stockton, Calif.: Instituto Fe y Vida, 2007), p. 39.

[61]Two examples of such programs described in chapter five include "The Master's Commission" at New Life Covenant Church in Chicago and the "Urban Training Centers" established by Victory Outreach International.

[62]Eldín Villafañe, *Seek the Peace of the City: Reflections on Urban Ministry* (Grand Rapids: Eerdmans, 1995), pp. 77-96.

naturally from the argument and the churches described in this book. But before commending this study humbly and prayerfully to my people *(mi gente)*, it is important to catch a glimpse of the Hispanic evangelical church's future through the eyes of visionary church leaders from across the country. As you will see, their visions often include the Hispanic church's future in the larger drama of God's mission *beyond* the barrio.

CONCLUSION

A FUTURE FOR THE LATINO CHURCH

The gifts [Christ] gave were that some would be apostles, some prophets,
some evangelists, some pastors and teachers, to equip the saints for the work
of ministry, for building up the body of Christ, until all of us come to the
unity of the faith and of the knowledge of the Son of God,
to maturity, to the measure of the full stature of Christ.

EPHESIANS 4:11-13

THE HISPANIC CHURCH MUST LOOK *within* and *beyond* the barrio to see its future in the mission of God. First, we must recognize the untapped resources within our communities and churches. Second, we must recognize that we are also uniquely positioned to be God's missionary people in a multiethnic, multilingual and multicultural America. With regard to the former we need to embrace the transgenerational nature of Hispanic ministry. With regard to the latter we must embrace our uniqueness as mestizo people in a world where, according to Virgilio Elizondo, "the future is mestizo."[1]

TRANSGENERATIONAL HISPANIC MINISTRY

When we look to the Scriptures for guidance with what Samuel Rodríguez calls "trans-generational Hispanic ministry," we discover an

---

[1]Virgilio Elizondo, *The Future Is Mestizo: Life Where Cultures Meet,* rev. ed. (Boulder: University of Colorado Press, 2000).

analogous context in the lives of the patriarchs.[2] Church leaders and members of Hispanic churches can learn much from the nature of God's interaction with Abraham, Isaac and Jacob. For instance, the call of Abraham serves as a decisive turning point or moment of transition in the moral history of humanity. Like many first-generation Latinos in the United States, Abraham was forced to leave his homeland and live as a "resident alien" in the land of Canaan, where his faith and trust in God were tested again and again. He was reassured by God that he would be blessed and that through him (i.e., his offspring) all the families and all the nations of the earth would be blessed (Gen 12:1-3; 22:18). When Isaac is born, Abraham teaches his son to rely wholeheartedly on God even in the most trying of circumstances (e.g., Gen 22:8). Shortly after Abraham dies, God confirms the transgenerational nature of the so-called Abrahamic promise to Isaac (Gen 26:4). It is here that Hispanic church leaders can learn an all-important lesson.

Isaac not only blesses his son Jacob, he also serves as a "bridge person" between Abraham and Jacob, that is, between the first and third generation. Isaac asks God to give his son Jacob "the blessing of Abraham," that is, the blessing of the immigrant generation. Even more, he asks God to give Abraham's blessing to Jacob's "offspring," that is, to the fourth generation (Gen 28:3-4). Shortly thereafter, God answers Isaac's prayer when he appears to Jacob in a dream at Bethel. Once again the Lord confirms the transgenerational nature of the promises made earlier to Abraham and Isaac (Gen 28:13-14).

Many years later, Jacob blesses his sons including Ephraim and Manasseh, the sons of Joseph, thereby continuing the legacy passed down to him from his father and grandfather (Gen 49:1-28). Thereafter the names of Abraham, Isaac and Jacob appear together frequently in the Old Testament, such as when the Lord identifies himself to Moses at the burning bush (Ex 3:16) and to the groaning Israelites before commencing the plagues upon Egypt (Ex 6:3). In the New Testament, the Lord Jesus Christ declares that it is none other than the God of Abraham, Isaac and Jacob that is present and acting

---

[2]Samuel Rodríguez, interview with author, December 10, 2009.

in his ministry (Mt 8:11). And the names of the patriarchs also appear together in the book of Acts, most notably when Peter is preaching in the temple (Acts 3:13).

The point that must not escape us is that at significant turning points in the history of redemption, the Lord binds parent, child and grand-child together through a common blessing and promise. Abraham's blessing and promise is also Isaac's. Isaac's blessing and promise belongs to Jacob as well. And Jacob's blessing and promise is passed on to his sons and grandsons alike. When we fast-forward almost two thousand years, Paul declares "if you belong to Christ, then you are Abraham's offspring, heirs according to the promise" (Gal 3:29). If like Isaac and Jacob we are "heirs of the promise" to bless "all the families of the earth," it behooves us to begin with our own families! We must start by passing the blessings and promises of God given to *nuestros abuelitos* (our grandparents) and *nuestros padres* (our parents) to our children and grandchildren!

As we have observed in this study, the temptation to neglect the spiritual welfare of our U.S.-born English-dominant children and grandchildren can be more intense than we imagine. This is especially true if caring for the spiritual welfare of our children and grandchildren requires us to adapt our approaches and styles of ministry to "accom-modate" them rather than insisting that they worship and serve God according to our linguistic and cultural preferences. As the spiritual descendents of Abraham (Gal 3:29), it is incumbent upon us to follow the example of the patriarchs. We too are called to look out for the spiritual well-being of others. "Let each of you look not to your own interests, but to the interests of others" (Phil 2:4).

Second-generation Latinos are the key. Samuel Rodríguez urges His-panic church leaders "to invest in Isaac, he is the bridge between Abra-ham and Jacob's generation."[3] Second-generation Latinos can serve as a cultural as well as linguistic bridge between the first and third genera-tion. As we observed, studies have shown that second-generation Lati-nos are more likely than the first or the third generation to be bilin-

---

[3]Ibid.

gual.[4] Furthermore, their intimate relationship with each generation gives second-generation Latinos a unique advantage in bridging the so-called generation gap. Second-generation Latinos generally understand and appreciate the culture and the values of their foreign-born parents better than their third-generation children. They also understand the culture and the values of their third-generation children better than their foreign-born parents.

This dynamic has been seen multiple times in this study.[5] Second-generation Hispanic pastors including Isaac Canales, Danny de Leon, Víctor Rodríguez and Wilfredo De Jesús have each lead their respective churches through moments of transition that successfully transformed Spanish-only churches into multigenerational, multilingual congregations where foreign-born Latinos who speak little or no English *se sienten a gustos* (feel at ease) and where native-born Latinos who speak little or no Spanish also feel welcomed and accepted. Like Isaac, these visionary and courageous pastors are literally giving U.S.-born Latinos the "blessing of Abraham," that is, the blessing of intimately interacting with foreign-born Latinos under the same roof in multigenerational, multilingual Hispanic churches. More importantly, second-generation Hispanic leaders are helping to pass on the legacy of culture, language and faith to third and later generations of Latinos and even to non-Latinos.

The blessings of Abraham. The bilingual and bicultural nature of the majority of second-generation Latinos gives them many invaluable insights into both parent cultures, Latino and American. For example, Ed Morales asserts that "just being bilingual sheds light on *language* itself, the fact that it has structure. When one grows up monolingual, one may never understand language's abstract structure. The same goes for culture. The same goes for race."[6] More significantly, the bilingual and bicultural Isaac generation still appreciates the many gifts Abraham's generation (i.e., the foreign born) brought with them from our

---

[4]Pew Hispanic Center and Kaiser Family Foundation, "2002 National Survey of Latinos" (Washington, D.C.: Pew Hispanic Center, December 2002), p. 45.
[5]See chapter two of this study for relevant case studies.
[6]Ed Morales, *Living in Spanglish: The Search for Latino Identity in America* (New York: St. Martin's Press, 2002), p. 278.

ancestral homelands—gifts many of our people, especially those of us born in the United States, fail to recognize, value and claim as our inheritance. Chief among these gifts is what Mexican essayist Carlos Fuentes calls *"el sentido del sagrado"* (a "deep sense of the sacred"). This is nothing less than the "recognition that the world is holy, which is the oldest and deepest certitude of the Amerindian world."[7] Even though few of them knew the old Protestant hymn, our ancestors, perhaps more deeply than we do, understood "this is my Father's world." Our *abuelos'* inherent respect for the created order is manifest in their fascination with their urban gardens, an idiosyncrasy that was depicted beautifully in Gregory Nava's film *Mi Familia* (1995), starring Jennifer Lopez, Edward James Olmos and Jimmy Smits. Native-born Latinos, like Americans in general, are only recently becoming aware of the way humankind is destroying the planet that we were entrusted by God to protect as stewards. So it behooves us to claim this *sentido del sagrado* brought to us by the first generation, especially those from rural Mexico, Central America and the Caribbean, *la gente del campo* (the people of the countryside).

In order to appreciate the *sentido del sagrado* and other blessings of the immigrant generation, we must also acknowledge their care and respect for elders, "something called *respeto*—respect for experience and continuity, less than awe at change and novelty."[8] It is more than respect for age; it is respect for the stories and memories of our parents and grandparents. For Latino evangelicals, this includes the lessons they have learned along the road to Emmaus (Lk 24:13-35), where the risen Lord has journeyed with them expounding the truth about himself revealed in the Scriptures and in the disappointing and even painful events of their lives here in exile.

Many Isaacs among us, including second-generation Hispanic pastors, recognize the importance of modeling for younger Latinos the respectful attitude toward the first-generation that is becoming *un*characteristic of many third-generation Latinos in our society. Consci-

---

[7]Carlos Fuentes, *The Buried Mirror: Reflections on Spain and the New World* (New York: Houghton Mifflin, 1992), pp. 346-47.
[8]Ibid., p. 347.

entious Hispanic pastors do this publically and consistently to ensure a blessing for the younger generations. "Children, obey your parents in the Lord, for this is right. 'Honor your father and mother'—this is the first commandment with a promise: 'so that it may be well with you and you may live long on the earth'" (Eph 6:1-3).

One of the best examples of this respectful posture toward the first generation is that of Pastor Wilfredo De Jesús, a second-generation Puerto Rican whose leadership was instrumental in turning a small Spanish-speaking Pentecostal congregation into a five-thousand-member multigenerational and multiethnic predominately Hispanic megachurch, New Life Covenant Church in Chicago. De Jesús insists that initial fears, resistance and reluctance to agree with his proposed changes were diminished by the trust and confidence he earned during twenty years of faithful and loyal service to the church and to Pastor Ignacio Marrero, his Puerto Rican–born mentor and predecessor. Pastor Ignacio Marrero and other first-generation Hispanic leaders continue to be shown the utmost respect at New Life Covenant Church, where Pastor De Jesús serves as a bridge between foreign-born and native-born Latinos.[9]

First-generation Hispanics have also bequeathed to the generation of Isaac and Jacob an appreciation for and commitment to *la familia*.[10] They have taught us the value of fighting to keep the family together and of "providing a security net in times of trouble." This dedication to family also helps our people avoid what Carlos Fuentes refers to as "the poverty of loneliness."[11] Justo González argues that it is this appreciation for the family that prompts many Hispanic pastors to emphasize those biblical texts "having to do with the household or family of God" (see Gal 6:10; Eph 2:19-20; and 1 Tim 3:14-15).[12] Fortunately, our experience and social science research indicates that across generations,

---

[9]Wilfredo De Jesús, interview with author, May 23, 2008.

[10]This value was reinforced repeatedly and eloquently in *Rain of Gold*, the 1991 *New York Times* bestseller by Victor Villaseñor, which tells the story of the author's parents who immigrated to the United States from Mexico during the Mexican Revolution (1910-1917).

[11]Fuentes, *Buried Mirror*, p. 347.

[12]Justo L. González, *Santa Biblia: Reading the Bible Through Hispanic Eyes* (Nashville: Abingdon, 1996), p. 107.

Hispanic families are more inclined to maintain a strong sense of what Carlos Carrillo calls *"familismo"* even after they have assimilated in many other respects. Family pride and solidity "often serve as buffers against some of the negative effects of acculturation for Latino/a adolescents."[13]

More and more, people in the United States are starting to appreciate the advantages of speaking more than one language. Here too the first generation has preserved and offered to us the gift of our ancestral language, Spanish. In fact, despite the phenomenal growth of the native-born Latino population and its preference for English, experts including first-generation Mexican Ilian Stavans contend that unlike other ethnic groups, "Latinos are amazingly loyal to their mother tongue. Because of the geographic closeness of the countries of origin and the diversity of the composition of their communities, Spanish remains a unifying force, used at home, in school, and on the streets."[14] If this observation is accurate, it draws attention to important questions raised by Carlos Fuentes: "Is monolingualism unifying and bilingualism disruptive? Or is monolingualism sterile and bilingualism fertile?"[15]

The value of biculturalism and bilingualism. Before discussing the value of bilingualism and biculturalism, a point of clarification is in order. Thus far I have made the case that in an effort to win and retain the native-born generations for Christ, Hispanic evangelical churches in the United States must challenge the assumption that Hispanic ministry is synonymous with Spanish-language ministry. I have also challenged the assumption held by many that it is the Hispanic church's responsibility to preserve and reinforce Hispanic culture and the Spanish language, especially when this is done at the expense of native-born English-dominant Latinos. When native-born Latinos feel forced to speak Spanish in church and then are ridiculed for speaking it poorly, the Hispanic church is only hurting itself and risking alienating many

---

[13]Carlos Carrillo, "Faith and Culture in Hispanic Families," in *Pathways of Hope and Faith Among Hispanic Teens,* ed. Ken Johnson-Mondragón (Stockton, Calif.: Instituto Fe y Vida, 2007), p. 116.

[14]Ilan Stavans, *The Hispanic Condition: The Power of a People,* 2nd ed. (New York: HarperCollins, 2001), p. 153.

[15]Fuentes, *Buried Mirror,* p. 347.

second- and third-generation Latinos. Instead, I have argued that the church must willingly and strategically accommodate the linguistic and cultural preferences of U.S.-born Latinos. In many cases, this will result in the formation of multigenerational and multilingual Hispanic congregations. Nevertheless, for their own well-being I also believe we should encourage English-dominant Latinos to embrace their ancestral language and culture. However, we must do so without ridiculing them or inadvertently making them feel marginalized if they refuse our advice and offer of assistance.

Experts in the social sciences have much to say concerning the value of bilingualism and biculturalism. In his review of the pertinent literature, social work expert Melvin Delgado insists that bicultural and bilingual Latinos enjoy several advantages over monocultural and monolingual Latinos. For example, in response to the identity crisis experienced by many Latinos as a result of the process of acculturation, Delgado observes that a positive ethnic identity can be achieved through the development of an "integrative identity," by which he means a bicultural and bilingual identity. Bicultural youth are able to draw on cultural capital from both mainstream and immigrant culture, which helps them to socially navigate their way through life in an increasingly multicultural society. Furthermore, Delgado insists that Latinos who enjoy the greatest educational success are those who embrace their bicultural heritage.[16]

Noteworthy in this regard are findings by Cynthia Feliciano, who found that bicultural and bilingual Asian and Latino students are less likely to drop out of school when compared to their English-only counterparts. These studies also suggest that biculturalism and bilingualism are nurtured when Latinos are exposed to immigrant culture and what Feliciano refers to as the "immigrant ethic," including an appreciation for the opportunities available in the United Stated relative to those in their homelands, high aspirations, a belief that hard work will be rewarded, and a respect for authority.[17] Fortunately, due to the consis-

---

[16]Melvin Delgado, *Social Work with Latinos: A Cultural Assets Paradigm* (Oxford: Oxford University Press, 2007), pp. 116-17.
[17]Cynthia Feliciano, "The Benefits of Biculturalism: Exposure to Immigrant Culture and

tently high rate of immigration from Latin American since 1980, the proportion of young Latinos who are children of immigrants is remarkably high.[18]

Here again, the example of denominational and local church leaders is indispensable. If we believe that biculturalism and bilingualism are valuable traits worth preserving and cultivating, we must embrace them ourselves as we encourage others to do so. This is what inspired Paul Flores, a second-generation Mexican American and pastor of Church of the Redeemer in Baldwin Park, California, to reengage his Latino roots, the Hispanic community and the Spanish language. Paul observed his father, Pastor Emeritus Aureliano Flores, struggle intentionally and strategically for more than a decade to become fluent in English and comfortable within the society of the dominant group. The effort allowed Paul's father to transform a small Spanish-only congregation dominated by immigrants into a thriving five-hundred-member multigenerational and multilingual Hispanic church. Paul Flores is now well on his way to becoming bilingual and bicultural. In the process he is inspiring and challenging other native-born members of his congregation to follow his example. Even more importantly, Paul Flores is also equipping and positioning himself to serve like Isaac as a bridge between the immigrant generation and the third generation, that is, between Abraham and Jacob. Another net result is the strong sense of "*familismo*" that crosses generational and linguistic boundaries at Church of the Redeemer.

HELLENISTS MAKE GREAT CROSSCULTURAL MISSIONARIES

My research has also helped me to recognize that U.S.-born English-dominant Latinos are not only "targets of mission," they are also "agents of mission." Once again lessons from the book of Acts are instructive. Luke observes that Hellenistic Jews (i.e., Greek-speaking Jews) are also effective missionaries, not only among fellow Jews but also among Sa-

---

Dropping out of School Among Asian and Latino Youths," *Social Science Quarterly* 82, no. 4 (2001): 877.

[18]Ken Johnson-Mondragón, *Pathways of Hope and Faith Among Hispanic Teens*, ed. Ken Johnson-Mondragón (Stockton, Calif.: Instituto Fe y Vida, 2007), p. 15.

maritans and Gentiles. Hellenistic Jews, especially those from the Diaspora, are among those who listen to Peter's sermon on the day of Pentecost (Acts 2:7-12).[19] From Acts 6:5 we know that Stephen, the first Christian martyr, and Philip "the evangelist" (Acts 21:8) are also Hellenists. Luke also tells his readers that as a result of the intense persecution associated with Stephen's murder, converted Hellenists from the Diaspora are among the first to intentionally reach out to "Greeks" in Antioch of Syria (Acts 11:19-21). The ability of these un-named "men of Cyprus and Cyrene" to see themselves not as refugees but as ambassadors for Christ reminds me of the proverb quoted often by our *abuelas* during difficult times, *"No hay mal que por bien no venga"* ("There is no bad from which good doesn't come"). Through the mis-sionary activity of these Greek-speaking Jewish Christians from Cyrus and Cyrene, "the good news of the Lord" begins to spread among Gen-tiles in important non-Jewish areas of the eastern Mediterranean in-cluding Antioch. And it is from Antioch, a church composed primarily of converted Greek-speaking Gentiles, that Paul and Barnabas are sent on their first missionary journey (Acts 13:1-3).

Of course Saul, "a Jew, from Tarsus in Cilicia" (Acts 21:39), and Barnabas, "a native of Cyprus" (Acts 4:36), were also originally from the Diaspora.[20] Like other Jewish Christians from the Diaspora, Paul and Barnabas were each uniquely qualified to bridge the linguistic, cultural and religious divide between the Jewish and Gentile worlds.[21] Whenever possible, Barnabas and Paul would proclaim "the word of God in the synagogue of the Jews" (Acts 13:5; 14:1; 17:1, 10, 17; 18:4; 19:8), where leaders would initially offer them the opportunity to preach for one or more sabbaths (Acts 13:15, 42; 18:4; 19:8). Frequently, the audience in the synagogue would include Greek proselytes referred to as "devout converts to Judaism" (Acts 13:43), as well as devout or

---

[19]For more information on the nature of Hellenistic Judaism, see Everett Ferguson, *Backgrounds of Early Christianity*, 3rd ed. (Grand Rapids: Eerdmans, 2003), pp. 428-29, 617-18.

[20]Like many Hellenized Jews, Saul and Barnabas had settled in Jerusalem. In the case of Saul, later known as Paul, it was to study under Gamaliel, the respected teacher of the law (Acts 5:34; 22:3; 26:4). See Luke T. Johnson, *The Acts of the Apostles* (Collegeville, Minn.: Liturgical Press, 1992), p. 108.

[21]See Eckhard J. Schnabel, *Paul the Missionary: Realities, Strategies and Methods* (Downers Grove, Ill.: InterVarsity Press, 2008), pp. 39-44.

"god-fearing Greeks" (Acts 17:4). The growing and enthusiastic crowds would cause the local Jewish leaders to become jealous and oppose the missionaries (Acts 13:45; 14:2; 17:5; 18:6). Rejected by the local Jewish leaders, Barnabas and Paul would leave the local synagogue accompanied by those who "were persuaded" (Acts 17:4) and "became believers" (Acts 14:1). Then, in obedience to the Lord (Acts 13:47), they would turn their attention and evangelistic efforts toward the Gentile community. Thus Hellenized Jews, Greek proselytes and devout or "god-fearing" Greeks who responded favorably to the gospel would then form the nucleus for a new multiethnic congregation.

Similarly, my research has revealed that U.S.-born English-dominant Latinos are not only a field "ripe for harvesting" (Jn 4:35), they are also the answer to the church's prayers that "the Lord of the Harvest" send out laborers into his harvest (Lk 10:2). Like Hellenized Jews in the first century, native-born Latinos are uniquely qualified to bridge the linguistic, cultural and religious divide between the Hispanic and non-Hispanic communities in the United States. As I demonstrated in chapter four, not only are U.S.-born English dominant Latinos planting and growing thriving Hispanic churches, they are also reaching beyond the barrio to plant and grow multiethnic churches across the country and around the world. In fact, they *are* actually nothing less than "a foretaste of the unity envisioned by God's love in Christ."[22]

CONCLUSION

Reminiscent of the writer of the third Gospel, I commend this study to *Theophilus*, that is, to those who are "lovers of God." For them I have "undertaken to set down an orderly account of the events that have been fulfilled among us" (Lk 1:1), that is, among Latino evangelicals in the early twenty-first century. My approach has been straightforward, to describe and analyze the cutting-edge ministry paradigms that one can observe in the barrio today, especially among native-born English-dominant Latinos in at-risk underserved communities. As an academic rather than a practitioner, I have been forced to rely heavily on partici-

---

[22]Harold J. Recinos, *Good News from the Barrio: Prophetic Witness for the Church* (Louisville, Ky.: Westminster John Knox, 2006), p. 107.

pant observations and interviews at Hispanic evangelical churches across the United States.

Like Luke's informants, "eyewitnesses and servants of the word" have graciously welcomed me into their lives and churches. U.S.-born Latino evangelicals have shared their stories with me, stories of marginalization and rejection by well-meaning but culturally insensitive foreign-born church leaders and members, who often appear to care more about preserving their culture and language than about sharing the gospel with the lost, even when the lost are their own children and grandchildren. But my gracious informants have also assisted me in writing "an orderly account" of the exciting ways the Lord is using them and a growing number of first-generation Hispanic pastors to reach multiple generations of Latinos, including native-born English-speaking Latinos who now dominate the Hispanic landscape in the United States.

My task has been made easier and personally more rewarding due to the hospitality and generosity of many first-generation Hispanic pastors whose examples I hope and pray many readers will emulate. The vision, courage and humility of first-generation Hispanic pastors including Aureliano Flores, Alberto Delgado, Luis Aranguren, Marc Rivera and Elieser Bonilla are by far the most exciting stories told in this book. Each of these pioneering church leaders embraces an all-important challenge raised earlier by Manuel Ortiz: to refuse to allow their linguistic or cultural comfort zones to determine the extent of their ministry.[23] Consequently, each of these pastors vigorously challenges the assumption that Hispanic ministry is synonymous with Spanish-language ministry.

Instead, these responsive first-generation Hispanic pastors attract and inspire second- and third-generation Latinos in their respective communities by humbly and courageously dedicating themselves to become all things to all Latinos, including those who speak little or no Spanish. The resulting paradigm shifts in their approaches to ministry demanded not just discipline and hard work; they also required great

---

[23]Manuel Ortiz, *The Hispanic Challenge: Opportunities Confronting the Church* (Downers Grove, Ill.: InterVarsity Press, 1993), p. 114.

humility as each struggled (and in some cases continue to struggle) to become fluent in English. Their commitment to become proficient in English and more knowledgeable about the socioeconomic and cultural context of native-born Latinos in the United States is driven by their desire to embrace the Great Commandment (Mk 12:29-31) as well as the Great Commission (Mt 28:18-20) and thereby provide pastoral care for every member of their congregation and community regardless of their linguistic or cultural preferences.

Thanks be to the God of our Lord and Savior Jesus Christ, today there are a growing number of churches across the United States that successfully reach native-born English-speaking Latinos who feel as though they are "trapped in the hyphen" between Latino and American. This is their story, the story of Hispanic churches that are becoming all things to all Latinos.

APPENDIX

Multigenerational/Multilingual Hispanic Churches
(in alphabetical order):

Iglesia Alpha & Omega/Alpha & Omega Church
Senior Pastor Alberto M. Delgado
Young Adult Pastor Mike Castillo
Website: http://alpha-omega.org
Address: 7800 SW 56th Street, Miami, FL 33155
Phone: (305) 273-1263

Iglesia del Redentor/Church of the Redeemer
Senior Pastor Paul Flores
Pastor Emeritus Aureliano Flores
Website: www.theredeemerchurch.org
Address: 3739 N. Monterey Ave., Baldwin Park, CA 91706
Phone: (626) 960-9585

Ministerios Coral Park/Coral Park Ministries
Senior Pastor Luis Aranguren
Website: www.coralpark.org
Address: 8755 SW 16th St., Miami, FL 33165
Phone: (305) 559-0241

Mission Ebenezer Family Church
Senior Pastor Isaac Canales
Website: www.missionebenezer.com
Address: 415 W. Torrance Blvd., Carson, CA 90745
Phone: (310) 329-9128

New Life Covenant Church
Senior Pastor Wilfredo De Jesús
Associate Pastor Pablo Chicol
Youth Pastor David Marrero
Website: mynewlife.org
Address: 2704 W. North Ave., Chicago, IL 60647
Phone: (773) 384-7113

Primitive Christian Church
Senior Pastor Marc Rivera
Associate Pastor David Morales
Website: www.primitivechurch.org
Address: 207-209 East Broadway, New York, NY 10002
Phone: (212) 673-7868

South San Filadelfia Church
Senior Pastor Victor Rodríguez
Website: www.myssfc.org
Address: 2483 W. Southcross Blvd., San Antonio, TX 78211
Phone: (210) 923-7759

Templo Calvario
Senior Pastor Daniel de Leon
Website: www.templocalvario.com
Address: 2617 W. 5th St., Santa Ana, CA 92703
Phone: (714) 834-9331

Thessalonica Christian Church
Pastor David Serrano
Address: 313 Saint Ann's Ave., Bronx, NY 10454
Phone: (718) 665-0182

Vida Abundante/Abundant Life Church of God
Senior Pastor Eliezer Bonilla
Website: www.abundant-life.cc
Address: 7431 S. Presa, San Antonio, TX 78233
Phone: (210) 532-7722

Multiethnic Predominantly Hispanic Churches
(in alphabetical order):

Calvary Chapel Montebello
Senior Pastor Pancho Juarez
Website: www.ccmtb.com
Address: 931 S. Maple Ave., Montebello, CA 90640
Phone: (323) 724-8464

Calvary Fellowship
Lead Pastor Bob Franquiz
Youth Pastor Mark Rodríguez
Website: www.calvarywired.com
Address: 5803 NW 151 St., Suite 207, Miami Lakes, FL 33014
Phone: (305) 822-7000

FaithWorld International Chicago
Senior Pastor Daniel Cruz
Pastor Alberto Guerrero
Youth Pastor Eddie León
Website: faithworldchicago.org
Address: 4047 West Fullerton Ave., Chicago, IL 60639-2136
Phone: (773) 489-7601

New Harvest Christian Fellowship
Senior Pastor Richard Salazar
Website: www.newharvestoneighty.com
Address: 11364 E. Imperial Highway, Norwalk, CA 90650
Phone: (562) 929-6034

Praise Chapel Christian Fellowship
Senior Pastor Donna Neville
Website: www.praisechapelhp.com
Address: 3034 E. Gage Ave., Huntington Park, CA 90255
Phone: (323) 589-8957

Victory Outreach International
Founding Pastor Sonny Arguinzoni
Website: www.victoryoutreach.org
Email: info@victoryoutreach.org
Address: P.O. Box 3760, San Dimas, CA 91773
Phone: (909) 599-4437

Waves of Faith
Lead Pastor Rey Martínez
Website: www.wavesoffaith.com
Address: 110 East Felix St., Fort Worth, TX 76115
Phone: (817) 926-6121

BIBLIOGRAPHY

Alba, Richard, John Logan, Amy Lutz and Brian Stults. "Only English by the Third Generation? Loss and Preservation of the Mother Tongue Among the Grandchildren of Contemporary Immigrants." *Demography* 39, no. 3 (2002): 467-84.

Arce, Carlos H. "A Reconsideration of Chicano Culture and Identity." *Daedulus* 110, no. 2 (1981): 171-91.

Arguinzoni, Sonny. *Sonny*. San Dimas, Calif.: Vision Multimedia, 1987.

————. *Internalizing the Vision*. San Dimas, Calif.: Vision Multimedia, 1995.

Arguinzoni, Sonny, and Julie Arguinzoni. *Treasures Out of Darkness*. San Dimas, Calif.: Vision Multimedia, 2000.

Baker, William R. *Evangelicalism & the Stone-Campbell Movement*. Downers Grove, Ill.: InterVarsity Press, 2002.

Bakke, Ray. *A Theology as Big as the City*. Downers Grove, Ill.: InterVarsity Press, 1997.

Bañuelas, Arturo J., ed. *Mestizo Christianity: Theology from a Latino Perspective*. Maryknoll, N.Y.: Orbis, 1995.

Bernal, Martha E., and George P. Knight, eds. *Ethnic Identity: Formation and Transmission Among Hispanics and Other Minorities*. New York: State University of New York, 1993.

Blea, Irene I. *Toward a Chicano Social Science*. New York: Praeger Paperback, 1988.

Bowker, John, ed. *The Oxford Dictionary of World Religions*. New York: Oxford University Press, 1997.

Brown, Dennis. "English Spoken Here? What the 2000 Census Tells Us About Language in the USA." Department of English, University of Illinois <www.english.illinois.edu/-people-/faculty/debaron/403/403readings /english%20spoken.pdf.>, p. 5.

Burgess, Stanley M., and Eduard M. Van Der Maas, eds. *The New International Dictionary of Pentecostal and Charismatic Movements*. Grand Rapids: Zondervan, 2002.

Camarillo, Albert M. and Frank Bonilla. "Hispanics in a Multicultural Society: A New American Dilemma?" In *America Becoming: Racial Trends and Their Consequences*. Edited by Neil J. Smelzer, William J. Wilson and Faith Mitchell, pp. 103-34. Washington, D.C.: National Academy Press, 2001.

Carrillo, Carlos. "Faith and Culture in Hispanic Families." In *Pathways of Hope and Faith Among Hispanic Teens*. Edited by Ken Johnson-Mondragón, pp. 113-59. Stockton, Calif.: Instituto Fe y Vida, 2007.

Chávez Sauceda, Teresa. "Becoming a Mestizo Church." In *¡Alabadle! Hispanic Christian Worship*. Edited by Justo L. González, pp. 89-99. Nashville: Abingdon, 1996.

Coleman, Robert. *The Master Plan of Evangelism*. Old Tappan, N.J.: Fleming H. Revell, 1963.

Conn, Harvie M. *The American City and the Evangelical Church: A Historical Overview*. Grand Rapids: Baker Academic, 1994.

———, ed. *Planting and Growing Urban Churches: From Dream to Reality*. Grand Rapids: Baker Academic, 1997.

Costas, Orlando E. *The Church and Its Mission: A Shattering Critique from the Third World*. Wheaton, Ill.: Tyndale House, 1974.

———. *The Integrity of Mission: The Inner Life and Outreach of the Church*. New York: Harper & Row, 1979.

———. *Christ Outside the Gate: Mission Beyond Christendom*. Maryknoll, N.Y.: Orbis, 1982.

———. "Evangelism from the Periphery: The Universality of Galilee." In *Voces: Voices from the Hispanic Church*. Edited by Justo L. González, pp. 16-23. Nashville: Abingdon, 1992.

Crespo, Orlando. *Being Latino in Christ: Finding Wholeness in Your Ethnic Identity*. Downers Grove, Ill.: InterVarsity Press, 2003.

Cruz, Nicky. *Give Me Back My Dignity*. La Puente, Calif.: Cruz Press, 1993.

Cuellar, Israel, Bill Arnold and Roberto Maldonado. "Acculturation Rating Scale for Mexican Americans-II: A Revision of the Original ARSMA Scale." *Hispanic Journal of Behavioral Sciences* 17 (1995): 257-304.

Cuellar, Israel, Bill Nyberg, Roberto Maldonado and Robert E. Roberts. "Ethnic Identity and Acculturation in a Young Adult Mexican-Origin Population." *Journal of Community Psychology* 25, no. 6 (1997): 535-49.

Darino, Miguel Angel. "What Is Different About Hispanic Baptist Worship?" In ¡Alabadle! Hispanic Christian Worship. Edited by Justo L. González, pp. 73-87. Nashville: Abingdon, 1996.

De La Torre, Miguel A., and Edwin David Aponte. Introducing Latino/a Theologies. Maryknoll, N.Y.: Orbis, 2001.

Delgado, Melvin. Social Work with Latinos: A Cultural Assets Paradigm. Oxford: Oxford University Press, 2007.

Douglas, J. D., ed. Let the Earth Hear His Voice: International Congress on World Evangelization, Lausanne, Switzerland. Minneapolis: World Wide Publications, 1975.

Dyck, Drew, Jon Rising and Joel Kilpatrick. "2007 Models in Innovation." Ministry Today (Mar/Apr 2007) <www.ministrytodaymag.com/display .php?id=14742>.

Elizondo, Virgilio P. "Mestizaje as a Locus of Theological Reflection." In Mestizo Christianity: Theology from a Latino Perspective. Edited by Arturo J. Bañuelas, pp. 5-27. Maryknoll, N.Y.: Orbis, 1995.

———. The Future Is Mestizo: Life Where Cultures Meet. Rev. ed. Boulder: University of Colorado Press, 2000.

———. Galilean Journey: The Mexican-American Promise. Rev. ed. Maryknoll, N.Y.: Orbis, 2000.

Ellison, Craig W. "Addressing the Felt Needs of Urban Dwellers." In Planting and Growing Urban Churches: From Dream to Reality. Edited by Harvie M. Conn, pp. 94-109. Grand Rapids: Baker Academic, 1997.

Elliston, Edgar J. Home Grown Leaders. Pasadena, Calif.: William Carey Library, 1992.

Elliston, Edgar J., and J. Timothy Kauffman. Developing Leaders for Urban Ministries. American University Studies, vol. 147. New York: Peter Lang, 1993.

Escobar, Samuel. The New Global Mission: The Gospel from Everywhere to Everyone. Downers Grove, Ill.: InterVarsity Press, 2003.

Espinoza, Gastón. "Victory Outreach International." In The New International Dictionary of Pentecostal and Charismatic Movements. Edited by Stanley M. Burgess and Eduard M. Van Der Maas, pp. 331-32. Grand Rapids: Zondervan, 2002.

Feliciano, Cynthia. "The Benefits of Biculturalism: Exposure to Immigrant Culture and Dropping out of School Among Asian and Latino Youths." Social Science Quarterly 82, no. 4 (2001): 865-79.

Ferguson, Everett. *Backgrounds of Early Christianity.* 3rd ed. Grand Rapids: Eerdmans, 2003.

———. *Baptism in the Early Church: History, Theology, and Liturgy in the First Five Centuries.* Grand Rapids: Eerdmans, 2009.

Ferris, Robert W. *Renewal in Theological Education: Strategies for Change.* Wheaton, Ill.: The Billy Graham Center, Wheaton College, 1990.

Fitzmyer, Joseph A. *The Acts of the Apostles.* New York: Doubleday, 1998.

Flores, Carlos. "Race Discrimination within the Latino Community." *Diálogo, Center for Latino Research DePaul University* 5 (Winter/Spring 2001): 30-32.

Fraga, Luis Ricardo, John A. Garcia, Rodney E. Hero, Michael Jones-Correa, Valerie Martínez-Ebers and Gary M. Segura. *Latino Lives in America: Making It Home.* Philadelphia: Temple University Press, 2010.

Fry, Richard, and Jeffrey S. Passel. "Latino Children: A Majority Are U.S.-Born Offspring of Immigrants." Washington, D.C.: Pew Hispanic Center, May 2008.

Fry, Richard. "Latino Settlement in the New Century." Washington, D.C.: Pew Hispanic Center, October 2008.

Fuentes, Carlos. *The Buried Mirror: Reflections on Spain and the New World.* New York: Houghton Mifflin, 1992.

Garcia, John A. "Ethnicity and Chicanos: Measurement of Ethnic Identification, Identity, and Consciousness." *Hispanic Journal of Behavioral Sciences* 4 (1982): 295-314.

Garcia, Jorge J. E. *Hispanic/Latino Identity: A Philosophical Perspective.* Malden, Mass.: Blackwell, 2000.

Garcia, Saul. *Semper Fidelis: The Character of a Leader.* San Dimas, Calif.: Vision Multimedia, 2005.

Gibbs, Eddie. *LeadershipNext: Changing Leaders in a Changing Culture.* Downers Grove, Ill.: InterVarsity Press, 2005.

González, Justo L. *Mañana: Christian Theology from a Hispanic Perspective.* Nashville: Abingdon, 1990.

———, ed. *Voces: Voices from the Hispanic Church.* Nashville: Abingdon, 1992.

———. *Santa Biblia: The Bible Through Hispanic Eyes.* Nashville: Abingdon, 1996.

———, ed. *¡Alabadle! Hispanic Christian Worship.* Nashville: Abingdon, 1996.

González, Robert O. "The New Evangelization and Hispanics in the United States." *America,* October 19, 1991, pp. 268-69.

Greenway, Roger S. "Getting David Out of Saul's Armor." In *The Urban Face of Mission: Ministering the Gospel in a Diverse and Changing World.* Edited by Manuel Ortiz and Susan S. Baker, pp. 225-38. Phillipsburg, N.J.: P & R Publishers, 2002.

Guzmán, Betsy. "The Hispanic Population" 2000 Census Brief, C2KBR/01-3. Washington, D.C.: U.S. Census Bureau, May 2001.

Hakimzadeh, Shirin and D'Vera Cohn. "English Usage Among Hispanics." Washington, D.C.: Pew Hispanic Center, November 2007.

Hall, Edward. *The Silent Language.* Garden City, N.Y.: Doubleday, 1973.

Harper, Nile. *Urban Churches, Vital Signs: Beyond Charity Toward Justice.* Grand Rapids: Eerdmans, 1999.

Hayes, Richard B. "The Letter of Paul to the Galatians." In *The Harper Collins Study Bible, Revised Edition.* Edited by Wayne A. Meeks, pp. 1972-74. New York: HarperCollins, 2006.

Heibert, Paul G. *Cultural Anthropology.* Grand Rapids: Baker, 1983.

Hernández, Edwin I. "Moving from the Cathedral to Storefront Churches: Understanding Religious Growth and Decline Among Latino Protestants." In *Protestantes/Protestants: Hispanic Christianity Within Mainline Traditions.* Edited by David Maldonado Jr., pp. 216-35. Nashville: Abingdon, 1999.

———. "The Religious Experience of Latino/a Protestant Youth." In *Pathways of Hope and Faith Among Hispanic Teens.* Edited by Ken Johnson-Mondragón, pp. 291-319. Stockton, Calif.: Instituto Fe y Vida, 2007.

Hughes, Richard T. *Myths America Lives By.* Urbana: University of Illinois Press, 2004.

Humes, Karen R., Nicholas A. Jones and Roberto R. Ramirez. "Overview of Race and Hispanic Origin: 2010." Washington, D.C.: U.S. Census Bureau, March 2011.

Hunter, James D. *American Evangelicalism: Conservative Religion and the Quandary of Modernity.* New Brunswick, N.J.: Rutgers University Press, 1983.

Huntington, Samuel P. *Who Are We? The Challenges to America's National Identity.* New York: Simon and Schuster, 2004.

International Consultation on the Relationship Between Evangelism and Social Responsibility. "Grand Rapids Report on Evangelism and Social Responsibility: An Evangelical Commitment." In *Making Christ Known: Historic Mission Documents from the Lausanne Movement, 1974-1989*. Edited by John Stott, pp. 165-213. Grand Rapids: Eerdmans, 1996.

Johnson, Luke T. *The Acts of the Apostles*. Collegeville, Minn.: Liturgical Press, 1992.

Johnson-Mondragón, Ken, ed. *Pathways for Hope and Faith Among Hispanic Teens: Pastoral Reflections and Strategies Inspired by the National Study of Youth and Religion*. Stockton, Calif.: Instituto Fe y Vida, 2007.

Juárez, Pancho. *An Altered Life*. Montebello, Calif.: Calvary Chapel of Montebello, 2005.

Keefe, Susan E., and Amado M. Padilla. *Chicano Ethnicity*. Notre Dame, Ind.: University of Notre Dame, 1987.

Kraft, Charles H. *Christianity and Culture*. Maryknoll, N.Y.: Orbis, 1981.

Knight, George P., and M. E. Bernal, M. K. Cota, C. A. Garza and K. A. Ocampo. "Family Socialization and Mexican American Identity and Behavior." In *Ethnic Identity: Formation and Transmission Among Hispanics and Other Minorities*. Edited by Martha E. Bernal and George P. Knight, pp. 105-29. New York: State University of New York, 1993.

Lausanne Movement. "The Lausanne Covenant." In *Making Christ Known: Historic Mission Documents from the Lausanne Movement, 1974-1989*. Edited by John Stott, pp. 1-55. Grand Rapids: Eerdmans, 1996.

———. "The Manila Manifesto." In *Making Christ Known: Historic Mission Documents from the Lausanne Movement, 1974-1989*. Edited by John Stott, pp. 225-49. Grand Rapids: Eerdmans, 1996.

Lingenfelter, Sherwood. *Ministering Cross-Culturally: An Incarnational Model for Personal Relationships*. 2nd ed. Grand Rapids: Baker Academic, 2003.

———. *Transforming Culture: A Challenge for Christian Mission*. 2nd ed. Grand Rapids: Baker Academic, 2004.

Maldonado, David, Jr., ed. *Protestantes/Protestants: Hispanic Christianity Within Mainline Traditions*. Nashville: Abingdon, 1999.

Martínez, Juan Francisco. *Walk with the People: Latino Ministry in the United States*. Nashville: Abingdon, 2008.

———. "Acculturation and the Latino Protestant Church in the United States." In *Los Evangélicos: Portraits of Latino Protestantism in the United States*. Edited by Juan F. Martínez and Lindy Scott, pp. 105-18. Eugene, Ore.: Wipf & Stock, 2009.

Martínez, Juan Francisco and Lindy Scott, eds. *Los Evangélicos: Portraits of La-*

tino Protestantism in the United States. Eugene, Ore.: Wipf & Stock, 2009.

Mayers, Marvin K. *Christianity Confronts Culture.* Grand Rapids: Zondervan, 1987.

Meeks, Wayne A., ed. *The HarperCollins Study Bible.* Rev. ed. San Francisco: HarperCollins, 2006.

Milne, Bruce. *The Message of John.* Downers Grove, Ill.: InterVarsity Press, 1993.

Morales, Ed. *Living in Spanglish: The Search for Latino Identity in America.* New York: St. Martin's Press, 2002.

Moyerman, David R., and Bruce D. Forman. "Acculturation and Adjustment: A Meta-Analytic Study." *Hispanic Journal of Behavioral Sciences* 14 (1992): 163-200.

Myers, Edward P. "Churches of Christ (A Capella), Are we Evangelical?" In *Evangelicalism and the Stone-Campbell Movement.* Edited by William R. Baker, pp. 50-69. Downers Grove, Ill.: InterVarsity Press, 2002.

National Youth Gang Center. "National Youth Gang Survey Analysis." Accessed on September 16, 2010 at <www.nationalgangcenter.gov>.

Negy, Charles, and Donald J. Woods. "The Importance of Acculturation in Understanding Research with Hispanic-Americans." *Hispanic Journal of Behavioral Sciences* 14 (1992): 224-27.

———. "A Note on the Relationship Between Acculturation and Socioeconomic Status." *Hispanic Journal of Behavioral Sciences* 14 (1992): 248-51.

Neville, Larry. *Connectivity: The Power to Touch the World.* Rancho Cucamonga, Calif.: Planters and Pioneers, 2006.

New American Dimensions. "Made in America: Communicating with Young Latinos." Accessed on November 8, 2008 at <www.newamericandimensions.com>.

Newbigin, Lesslie. *The Gospel in a Pluralistic Society.* Grand Rapids: Eerdmans, 1989.

Ortiz, Manuel. *The Hispanic Challenge: Opportunities Confronting the Church.* Downers Grove, Ill.: InterVarsity Press, 1993.

———. *One New People: Models for Developing a Multiethnic Church.* Downers Grove, Ill.: InterVarsity Press, 1996.

Ortiz, Manuel, and Susan S. Baker, eds. *The Urban Face of Mission: Ministering the Gospel in a Diverse and Changing World.* Phillipsburg, N.J.: P & R Publishers, 2002.

Padilla, Alvin. "Living in the Hyphen: Theological Literacy from an Hispanic American Perspective." In *Theological Literacy for the Twenty-First Century*. Edited by Rodney L. Petersen with Nancy M. Rourke, pp. 229-40. Grand Rapids: Eerdmans, 2002.

Passel, Jeffrey S., and D'Vera Cohn. "US Populations Projections 2005-2050." Washington, D.C.: Pew Hispanic Center, February 2008.

Pedraja, Luis. *Jesus Is My Uncle: Christology from a Hispanic Perspective*. Nashville: Abingdon, 1999.

Perl, Paul, Jennifer Z. Greely and Mark M. Gray. "How Many Hispanics Are Catholic? A Review of Survey Data and Methodology." Washington, D.C.: Center for Applied Research in the Apostolate Georgetown University, 2004.

Petersen, Rodney L., with Nancy M. Rourke, eds. *Theological Literacy for the Twenty-First Century*. Grand Rapids: Eerdmans, 2002.

Pew Hispanic Center. "A Statistical Portrait of Hispanics at Mid-Decade." Washington, D.C.: Pew Hispanic Center, September 2006.

———. "Changing Faiths: Latinos and the Transformation of American Religion." Washington, D.C.: Pew Hispanic Center, April 2007.

———. "Statistical Portrait of Hispanics in the United States, 2009." Washington, D.C.: Pew Hispanic Center, February 2011.

———. "Census 2010: 50 Million Latinos: Hispanics Account for More Than Half of Nation's Growth in Past Decade." Washington, D.C.: Pew Hispanic Center, March 2011.

Pew Hispanic Center and Kaiser Family Foundation. "2002 National Survey of Latinos." Washington, D.C.: Pew Hispanic Center, December 2002.

———. "Bilingualism." Washington, D.C.: Pew Hispanic Center, March 2004.

Pew Hispanic Center/Pew Forum on Religion and Public Life. "PEW 2006 U.S. Religion Survey." Washington, D.C.: Pew Hispanic Center, 2006.

Portes, Alejandro and Lingxin Hao. "E Pluribus Unum: Bilingualism and the Loss of Language in the Second Generation." *Sociology of Education* 71 (1998): 269-94.

Portes, Alejandro, and Ruben Rumbaut. *Legacies: The Story of the Immigrant Second Generation*. Berkeley: University of California Press, 2001.

Praise Chapel Christian Fellowship. *Policy Manual 2006*. Rancho Cucamonga, Calif.: Praise Chapel Christian Fellowship, 2006.

Ramírez, Johnny, and Edwin I. Hernández. *AVANCE: A Vision for a New Mañana*. Loma Linda, Calif.: Loma Linda University Press, 2003.

Recinos, Harold J. *Who Comes in the Name of the Lord? Jesus at the Margins.* Nashville: Abingdon, 1997.

———. *Good News from the Barrio: Prophetic Witness for the Church.* Louisville, Ky.: Westminster John Knox, 2006.

Riebe-Estrella, Gary. "A Youthful Community: Theological and Ministerial Challenges." *Theological Studies* 65 (2004): 314.

Roberts Gaventa, Beverly. *The Acts of the Apostles.* Nashville: Abingdon, 2003.

Rodríguez, Richard. *Hunger of Memory: The Education of Richard Rodriguez.* New York, Bantam Books, 1982.

Rueschenberg, Erich, and Raymond Buriel. "Mexican American Family Functioning and Acculturation: A Family Systems Perspective." *Hispanic Journal of Behavioral Sciences* 11 (1989): 232-42.

Sánchez, Daniel R. *Hispanic Realities Impacting America: Implications for Evangelism & Missions.* Fort Worth, Tex.: Church Starting Network, 2006.

Schaerer, Enrique. "Intragroup Discrimination." *Berkeley Electronic Press,* October 18, 2008.

Schnabel, Eckhard J. *Paul the Missionary: Realities, Strategies and Methods.* Downers Grove, Ill.: InterVarsity Press, 2008.

Schreiter, Robert J. *Constructing Local Theologies.* Maryknoll, N.Y.: Orbis, 1985.

Sider, Ronald J. *Good News and Good Works: A Theology for the Whole Gospel.* Grand Rapids: Baker, 1999.

Sider, Ronald J., Philip Olsson and Heidi Rolland Unruh. *Churches That Make a Difference.* Grand Rapids: Baker, 2002.

Simpkins, Ron. *The Harvest Generation: The Story of Praise Chapel.* Huntington Park, Calif.: Mission Global Harvest Press, 1994.

Smelzer, Neil J., William J. Wilson and Faith Mitchell, eds. *America Becoming: Racial Trends and Their Consequences.* Washington, D.C.: National Academy Press, 2001.

Solivan-Román, Samuel. "The Need for a North American Hispanic Theology." In *Mestizo Christianity: Theology from the Latino Perspective.* Edited by Arturo J. Bañuelas, pp. 44-52. Maryknoll, N.Y.: Orbis, 1995.

———. "Hispanic Pentecostal Worship." In *¡Alabadle! Hispanic Christian Worship.* Edited by Justo L. González, pp. 43-55. Nashville: Abingdon, 1996.

Stavans, Ilan. *The Hispanic Condition: The Power of a People.* New York: HarperCollins, 2001.

Stearns, Richard. *The Hole in Our Gospel.* Nashville: Thomas Nelson, 2010.

Stetzer, Ed. "The 2007 Outreach 100, America's Largest and Fastest-Growing Churches." *Outreach Magazine* 6 (Fall 2007): special ed.

Stott, John, ed. *Making Christ Known: Historic Mission Documents from the Lausanne Movement, 1974-1989.* Grand Rapids: Eerdmans, 1996.

Suro, Robert, and Jeffrey S. Passel. "The Rise of the Second Generation: Changing Patterns in Hispanic Population Growth." Washington, D.C.: Pew Hispanic Center, October 2003.

Tobar, Héctor. *Translation Nation: Defining a New American Identity in the Spanish-Speaking United States.* New York: Riverhead Books, 2005.

U.S. Census Bureau, Population Division, Ethnic & Hispanic Statistics Branch. "The Hispanic Population in the United States: 2008." Washington D.C.: U.S. Census Bureau, March 2008.

Van Rheenen, Gailyn. *Missions: Biblical Foundations and Contemporary Strategies.* Grand Rapids: Zondervan, 1996.

Villafañe, Eldín. *The Liberating Spirit: Toward an Hispanic American Pentecostal Social Ethic.* Grand Rapids: Eerdmans, 1993.

———. *Seek the Peace of the City: Reflections on Urban Ministry.* Grand Rapids: Eerdmans, 1995.

———. *Beyond Cheap Grace: A Call to Radical Discipleship, Incarnation and Justice.* Grand Rapids: Eerdmans, 2006.

Villaseñor, Victor E. *Rain of Gold.* New York: Random House, 1991.

Weber, David J. *Foreigners in their Native Land: Historical Roots of the Mexican Americans.* Rev. ed. Albuquerque: University of New Mexico Press, 2004.

Williams, Norma. *The Mexican American Family: Tradition and Change.* Dix Hill, N.Y.: General Hill, 1990.

Workforce Languages Services. "In Hiring, Hispanics Discriminate Against Other Hispanics." Chicago: Workforce Language Services (June 25, 2009).

Wright, Christopher J. H. *The Mission of God: Unlocking the Bible's Grand Narrative.* Downers Grove, Ill.: InterVarsity Press, 2006.

Name and Subject Index

Scripture Index